D0436743

By the same author
Patterns of Brief Family Therapy
Keys to Solution in Brief Therapy

A NORTON PROFESSIONAL BOOK

Clues

Clues

Investigating Solutions in Brief Therapy

Steve de Shazer
Director
Brief Family Therapy Center/
Wisconsin Institute on Family Studies
Milwaukee, Wisconsin

W. W. NORTON & COMPANY
New York   *London*

Published simultaneously in Canada by Penguin Books
Canada Ltd., 2801 John Street, Markham, Ontario L3R 1B4.

Printed in the United States of America.

Library of Congress Cataloging-in-Publication Data

De Shazer, Steve.
  Clues: investigating solutions in brief therapy.

  Bibliography: p.
  1. Psychotherapy, Brief. I. Title.
RC480.55.D38 1988   616.89′14   87-34799

ISBN 0-393-70054-2

W. W. Norton & Company, Inc., 500 Fifth Avenue, New York, N.Y. 10110
W. W. Norton & Company Ltd., 37 Great Russell Street, London WC1B 3NU

4 5 6 7 8 9 0

FOREWORD

Somehow, writing these forewords does not seem to get easier with practice. So it is tempting just to say "Steve de Shazer is at it again. Here is more of the same, so if you found his previous articles and books interesting and useful, this one is for you."

But even though that brief statement is appropriate and basically accurate, I cannot in good conscience leave it at that. There may be some potential readers who do not know what de Shazer has been up to before, to whom "more of the same" would convey no information. Others might take "more of the same" as a criticism, although I mean it positively here. So I must specify a bit more.

I do *not* mean that de Shazer is just being repetitive, saying the same things over again in different words. I do mean that he is pursuing similar interests further and by means that remain similar in general or in principle. But in doing so he (with the acknowledged help of various colleagues) has developed concepts and practices that are new or that are specified more fully or clearly than in his previous writings.

As I see it, de Shazer has been and remains primarily interested in attempting to define the essence of efficient psychotherapy, both intellectually and practically—that is, to produce a clear and concise (ideally, a minimal) specification of what brief therapy is about and the steps involved in doing it. In pursuing this end, his work is guided and bounded by two major principles, here apparently pushed toward their limits. First, the field of study is brief psychotherapy itself, viewed (rather anthropologically, perhaps?) as a delimited and focused kind of social interaction, consisting mainly of the statements made between a therapist and a client or clients in an interview room. The "real" or "outside" world of the client enters only as reports made within this setting. This might at first seem an extreme or unreasonable narrowing of scope. Yet it is scientifically reasonable in focusing solely on the observable data, and moreover is only an extension of a viewpoint commonly taken for granted – the prime example being that therapy starts from and is based on a *statement* of a complaint.

Second, there is de Shazer's focus on solutions – or, to be more consistent, statements of solutions – as the shared aim of therapist and client in the purposive interaction called psychotherapy. In the present work, the central and guiding question in review, discussion, and analysis of the data (recordings of therapy sessions) is always "Does a given sequence of statements by a client and a therapist lead toward a solution or not?"

The whole process of de Shazer's inquiry – though it has obviously involved a great amount of careful and detailed analysis – can be seen, at least in retrospect, as an exercise in pursuing the implications of these two basic conceptions. Surely one needs to consider the context in which a given statement or sequence leads toward a solution or does not? Of course – but this context itself consists of prior statements or sequences. Thus a chain of sequences may be built up, ultimately from the opening statement in therapy to a statement of solution. Is there one such chain, simple or branching, a different chain for every case, or an interrelated set of chains? These questions are investigated by comparison and contrast of data from a variety of cases, to identify similarities that form a basis for a more general characterization and differences that must be taken into account separately. Again, though, the analysis and synthesis are concerned with identification of types of statements and sequences, not diagnostic categories or the particular content of what is stated. This aspect of the work, especially, has leaned on the use of computerized model building. This may fascinate some and dishearten others, but in either case it is important to remember that the computer is only a tool which can be helpful in carrying out this complex task of analysis and synthesis.

What has come from a great deal of time and effort expended along these lines? In simplest terms, considerable progress toward construction of a general flow chart of efficient psychotherapy. In my view this has much theoretical and practical value – and even esthetic value, at least for those who, like Einstein, see beauty in order and simplicity. But read the book and judge for yourself.

— John H. Weakland
Palo Alto, January 1988

CONTENTS

INTRODUCTION

Writing *Keys to Solution in Brief Therapy* (de Shazer, 1985), my second book, was easier than writing *Patterns of Brief Family Therapy* (de Shazer, 1982b). In part this was true because I switched from using a typewriter to using a word processor, I had written one book already, and the model was simpler. Writing this third book, I naively thought, would be easier still (in part because I switched from a primitive word processing program on a slow computer to an advanced program on a computer with a hard disk). However, I was wrong.

In both *Keys* and *Patterns* the focal point of the therapy described was the tasks or clues to solution presented by the therapist at the end of the session. Although "change" has been seen as a constant process, therapy and therefore "therapeutic change" was seen as primarily related to tasks and the clients' reports of homework performance. If this punctuation is true at all of this book, it is certainly less so.

As my colleagues and I at the Brief Family Therapy Center (BFTC) continue to study solution development, we have been forced by our analyses to look more and more at the process of the interview. We found it was no longer enough to use our (perhaps overly) simple idea that the interview led to the intervention strategy and therefore the task. Clearly, there are solution related things that the client and therapist **do** during the session. When all goes well, these point to a task which simply says: *Now that you know what works, do more of it.*

When studying the intervention phase of the session, after the break, the record of what was said to the client can usually be kept verbatim on one piece of paper, and a brief sketch of the report in the following session is all that is needed to assess the usefulness of that part of the process. The compliment phase of the message addresses the idiosyncrasies of the session and the people concerned and was seen as setting the stage for the tasks. This, in fact, can be made simpler through the use of formula tasks which do not vary with each use and the team has control over what is *the same* from session to session. Therefore, both the original search and re-search are promoted by the availability of simple records.

For several reasons, I did not (and still do not) like this shift in focus, but our investigation of solution development forced it on me. This is the second time that one of our investigations has forced a major shift in our approach (see de Shazer, 1985). Such shifts are normal parts of any exploration process: one follows where the data lead. As Kuhn (1970) pointed out, anomalies develop and either they need to be re-described *within* a current theory or the theory needs to *change* so that a description is possible.

The linkage between what we do (practice) and how we talk about or describe what we do (theory) is very strong (and recursive) and both of these (theory and practice) are recursively related to our ongoing research. This is part of our design or plan for our research and theory construction program. To avoid muddle and confusion: Theory, as I use the term, is not meant as an "explanation," but rather as a coherent "description" of specific sequences of events within a specific context.

Let's face it, interviews are a mess and therefore studying them is at least equally messy. At times there are 2, 3, 4, 5, or 6 people conversing in the therapy room: It is tough to tell chaos from confusion. The chaos increases when the therapist converses with more than one person and the team gets involved (randomly) via the phone and/or planfully through the break and the message at the close of the session.

When first you look at interviews it is the differences that stand out. Each member of the BFTC team has a different style and a different way of implementing the model. Eve Lipchik has a unique interviewing style, Insoo Kim Berg has another, Elam Nunnally has yet another, but they are clearly related to Insoo's (at least in regard to the number of words that the therapist uses and in regard to the amount of activity during the session). Wallace Gingerich's style, when compared to Eve's, Insoo's, and Elam's, is starkly minimal and closely related to mine. Ron Kral's style, when conversing with a family is clearly related to Insoo's but, when working with a couple or a single person, his style becomes more minimal, more clearly related to mine. Kate Kowalski's style is a minimal version of Elam's, etc. My interviewing style, (I've been told), is sparse, minimal, and simple. Of the group, I use the fewest number of words (per session) and I deliberately make a lot of use of silence. And yet, each member of the team will say that we are "*doing the same thing!*"

Curiously, the shift in focus from the formula tasks and other tasks at the end of the interview to the interviews themselves began with a formula task at the beginning of the interview. A chance event (an anomaly?) started it off. Two weeks in a row the same team observed first sessions during which the client spontaneously mentioned a change in the problem area that had happened in the days immediately prior to the session. Once the client brought it up, the therapist quickly moved into second session behavior, i.e., investigating and promoting change that had already happened. We organized a small project to look at "pre-therapy change" (Weiner-Davis, de Shazer and Gingerich, 1987) and found that, when immediately asked at the very beginning of the first session, clients will report "pre-therapy change" rather frequently. Since change had already happened, how could we do our job which, at that time, we saw as "initiating change"?

At about the same time, one day when I came behind the mirror during a first session, Wally Gingerich asked me "How do you know what to ignore?" Obviously, therapists make many decisions during a single session about what is important and what is not. Trying to answer this question led us to doing some process research on therapeutic interaction (de Shazer, Gingerich and Weiner-Davis, 1985; Gingerich, de Shazer and Weiner-Davis, 1987). During this research we saw (from analysis of coded interviews) "second session behavior" move into the first session as the therapists at BFTC focused more and more on what has become known as "exceptions to the rules of the problem."

Obviously, I am not suggesting that it is *either* look at the task-response pattern *or* look at the interview phase of the session. The tasks given to clients as homework are now, more clearly than before, related to the interview. In fact, one could go further: Which task to give is dependent on or determined by how client and therapist construct the interview. All that I am suggesting is that how the interview is constructed is the way currently know what to do.

As we looked at interviewing, we were – of course – fascinated by the questions (and comments) therapists devise to meet the purpose of the interview (Lipchik, 1987; Lipchik and de Shazer, 1986). However, as a way to organize a study of interviewing (for theory construction purposes), such a textual focus would involve either linguistics or literary criticism and thus would result in a complicated and tangled model reflecting the overwhelming variation in interviews[1]. Subsequently, the scheme we devised has proved itself useful in training therapists once they grasp the basic underlying pathways of the interview: a theory of solution.

PATHWAYS

Trying to specify what exactly happens during an interview led Wally Gingerich and me, joined by Hannah Goodman[2], to develop an expert system (a computer program) to

---

[1]Approaching the interview as a text or a script might, in fact, obfuscate matters making it difficult if not impossible to see the underlying principles.

[2]Hannah Goodman (at the time) Master's Candidate, Computer Sciences, University of Wisconsin-Milwaukee.

simulate the team (Goodman, 1986) and in the project's second phase we were joined by Peter Kim[3] and Jaeho Kim[4]. Simultaneously with the start of the expert system project, Alex Molnar and I (Molnar and de Shazer, 1987), studying a series of videotapes, began to abstract a map by looking at the therapist's tasks; this map has since been revised over and over. The version of the theory presented here is closely related to computer programs' architecture and to the tasks of the interview but it is highly distinct from both. In any event, the theory describes the various pathways from "complaint" to "goal achievement" and "solution" that cases predictably tend to follow. For instance, when the client has done *this*, it will predictably be followed by the therapist doing *that*, which will predictably be followed by the client's doing something that is one member of a class of possible responses and not something from some other possible classes of response. I am, however, solely responsible for this version and for the theoretical thinking and interpretation of the diagrammatic or graphic representation of the theory, colloquially known simply as the CENTRAL MAP.

As a result, the structure or family tree that we have developed for looking at interviews has given us a tool for disciplined observation and description of the resemblances among interviews in spite of their apparent diversity. This has helped me in my theory construction project which, in turn, has helped us to understand what it is we do.

There are several advantages that have come out of investigating the interviewing mess:

(1) The model is, in fact, rather simple in a different way. The therapist's primary tasks are performed during the interview itself. This means that there is less dependence in the model on the client being assigned

---

[3]Peter Kim, (at the time) Doctoral Candidate, Electrical Engineering-Computer Science Department, Marquette University, Milwaukee, Wisconsin.
[4]Jaeho Kim, Electrical Engineering-Computer Science Department, Marquette University, Milwaukee, Wisconsin.

homework tasks. Obviously, this makes brief therapy more flexible and more adaptable to other settings such as residential treatment facilities or inpatient units of psychiatric hospitals.

From an administrative and management perspective, brief therapy is a cost effective approach and, in these days of the HMO and EAP and other cost containment devices (including new insurance company limits), it is important that what brief therapists do is not just "less of the same" but is an approach designed to be both brief and effective.

(2) The greater majority of the time, the tasks that are given are already within the clients' experience and repertoire. This makes therapist-client cooperation not only easier but such a cooperative relationship develops naturally out of the construction of the interview. Thus, in a great many cases, designing tasks is simplified to telling clients to do more of something they are already doing.

(3) In a great many cases, the construction of the interview prompts clients to "see through" their framing of the problematic situation. This means that the harried therapist does not have to figure out what kind of reframe might be useful. The purpose of a reframing has already been met when clients see through their frame making fluke "exceptions" into differences that make a difference. This again minimizes the necessity for between-session behavioral tasks and makes brief therapy more viable in inpatient settings.

(4) The focus on the construction of the interview and the therapist's tasks within the session more clearly describes what therapist and client *do* that is useful in solution development. This makes it clearer just exactly how to do this approach without a team behind a mirror and the other accoutrements of a research, theory construction, and training institute.

(5) The theory and the model deal just with doing thera-

py within therapy's natural environment. It is up to the therapist and client to decide what the boundaries of that environment are. The theory has nothing whatsoever to say about "problems, complaints, difficulties" etc. In fact, the theory explicitly neither includes nor excludes ideas about causation and neither includes nor excludes the various ideas about problem maintainance: it only deals with doing therapy.

(6) And last, but far from least, the conversations with clients are frequently fun for therapist and client alike. A lot of humor develops spontaneously during the session as befuddled therapist helps bewildered client figure out what happens when the complaint does not and when the therapist (fitting with a rather general client frame) ingenuously asks "Suppose there was a miracle and this problem was solved. . . . "

THE CASE EXAMPLES

Throughout the book cases have been used to illustrate a theory of solution. They are not meant as a proof of the theory. Theories cannot be proved; they can only be proved to be not applicable under certain conditions. The cases chosen cover a wide range of complaints, involving various socio-economic classes. Some cases involved the use of a team (in the research and theory construction setting) and others were done solo (as a means of showing how to apply the theory in therapy's natural setting).

ACKNOWLEDGMENTS

No book is written in complete isolation and this is certainly true when the context in which a book is written is a research/theory-construction program, clinic and training organization like the Brief Family Therapy Center.

I first of all want to thank the members of the team for their contributions:

Insoo Kim Berg,

Wally Gingerich,

Eve Lipchik,

Elam Nunnally,

Kate Kowalski,

Ron Kral, and

Alex Molnar.

To a greater or lesser extent, each of them played a role in some or all phases of the book. It is safe to say that without them, nothing in this book would have been possible. They have put up with listening to me and have given me careful responses to the questions I posed. I wish to thank them in particular for forcing me to be more clear.

Hannah Goodman, Jaeho Kim, and Peter Kim (who have written the computer programs known as BRIEFER I and II) forced me to look at what specifically we do when following clues toward finding and/or constructing a solution.

I also want to thank the office staff, Dolores Van Erden (who has been with BFTC almost since the start), Judy (Van Erden) Parker, and Ruthann Galarza for keeping the rest of the world under control while I wrote.

John H. Weakland deserves a special thanks for his continuing support and encouragement. And continued thanks to Lyman Wynne.

And I wish to thank the participants in the many work-shops I have presented for their patience and kindness. Their questions have helped me clarify things and some of their suggestions have been included in this presentation unfortunately without citation.

1

SOLUTION FOCUS

Our solution-focused model (de Shazer, 1985) has continued to develop based on our experiences at the Brief Family Therapy Center. As we came to focus on solution development with more and more rigor and discipline, our study transformed both our method and our theory of solution. The underlying philosophy has not changed, but what we have learned has changed how we go about doing therapy. These changes are clearly developments of characteristics that have been part of our approach all along, only what we choose to focus on has changed.

TRANSFERABILITY

For instance, at BFTC we have been interested for many years in the transferability of interventions, particularly homework tasks, from one case to another. This focus has provided us with several clues toward better understanding the processes of solution development. Previous work, focused on "problem solving" (de Shazer, 1982b, 1984; de Shazer and Molnar, 1984), suggested that the transfer of some tasks depends on the clients' interactional patterns (i.e., assigning a structured fight to stop couples' arguing) while others depend on the clients' frame or the definition of the complaint (i.e., assigning writing to replace "obsessive thoughts").

More recent work, focused on "solution development" (de

Shazer 1985), suggests that transferability, in some cases, depends more on the structure of the task itself and has little or nothing to do with the interactional patterns or the specific frame of a particular complaint (i.e., telling the client to "do something different" in the problematic situation). This type of transferable task is referred to as a "skeleton key." Another example is our Formula First Session Task (FFST):

> *"Between now and next time we meet, we would like you to observe, so that you can describe to us next time, what happens in your family that you want to continue to have happen."* (de Shazer, 1985, p. 137)

which does not even depend on either client or therapist being able to describe what the problem is. Frequently in the following session the client will report having done something or having had something happen that is clearly different. Skeleton keys seem useful in opening the door to change and solution in many situations regardless of the specific complaint involved.

During this period, our description pivoted on the task assignment from one session and the clients' report in the following session. This focus on the transferability of tasks has trained us to observe and describe patterns or sequences of events. From case to case and session to session, these patterns can be seen as similar in the same way that a musical variation is similar to its theme. After years and years of watching sessions from behind the mirror and/or watching videotapes of sessions, what stands out is the sameness. One session looks much like another no matter how different the content and the people involved.

MARKING DIFFERENCES

This sameness is useful, perhaps necessary, because it prepares the observer to notice anything different. Once something different is noticed, then the excitement builds again as the observers look for similar events and patterns. When a new pattern is described, then the observers need to figure out if this difference is of the kind that makes a difference. If so, then our methods of description will change along with the change in what it is that we describe. As a consequence, the expression of a theory will also change although the general theoretical conditions remain the same.

Behind the mirror, we describe our observations of a session or a series of sessions (in the same case) and search through our memories (and videotapes) of previous cases and unrelated sequences of events that fit the same rules for describing patterns and form. This process of comparison allows us to study the patterns and forms of interaction and relationship involved in various situations, clinical and otherwise. That is, sessions and cases are compared *through* the patterns and forms of the *descriptions* rather than the more traditional approach of comparing cases through the medium of the complaint pattern or the "symptom" or the "disease." Simply, what is observable, repeatable, and communicable is the patterns and forms of our descriptions.

To illustrate, Mr. Jones (A) who wants to lose weight and – on particular days eats in ways destined to reduce weight – would be compared with Mrs. Smith (B) who wants her child to behave better in school – and on particular days the child does behave quite well – rather than with Mr. Black (C) who wants to lose weight – and does not do anything about it. Furthermore, if the therapist working with Mr. Jones spent 30 minutes trying to help him describe days when he ate well but this process took only 7 minutes with Mrs. Smith, then Jones's case might also be compared with that of Miss White (D) who also took longer to describe those rare times when she did meet men.

When the pattern and form of the descriptions are similar (A to B, A to D, B to D, etc.), the process of comparison leads to the idea that the same intervention might be useful in kindred cases, i.e., keys and skeleton keys. If we told the client in cases B and D to "observe what happens that they

want to see continue to happen" and they did while reporting steps toward solution, then giving the client in case A
the same task might lead toward solution.

As we continued to observe this process we turned our
focus to the interviewing process when we noticed how
many clients reported exceptions to the rule that the complaint always happens. Some of these exceptions the clients
described as *spontaneous* – "it just happened" – while others
they described as the result of a *deliberate* shift in behavior.
In either case, their description can be seen as including a
difference that had not yet made a difference to them. Our
belief in the constancy of the process of transformation or
change was given a further boost.

This new pattern in our descriptions led to the invention
of a new skeleton key: *searching for exceptions*[1] *that could
be made into differences that make a difference.* (This key is
logically identical with our Formula First Session Task (de
Shazer, 1985) and its variations.) When this search is successful and differences are observed and talked about in the
first session, the expectation of *significant* transformation
in the area of the complaint, as well as of a solution, is
affirmed for both therapist and client because something
different has already happened in the area of the complaint!
Since the client is already doing something about the complaint, therapist-client cooperation is assured when this success becomes the therapist's focus. This, understandably,
means that the therapist is, already in the first session,
responding with an *open* expectation of *continuing* transformation or change.

Previously, when our focus was on those keys which we

---

[1]The term "exception" is used because clients tend to view their complaints
or problems as "always happening" (a rule). When the complaint does not
happen, it is as if a rule had been broken but that change is not seen as
significant. The non-occurrence of the problem is seen as "a fluke" rather
than as evidence that things might be getting better, suggesting that "every rule has an exception."

The term "exception" readily fits the clients' point of view or at least the
therapist's view of the clients' view.

used as interventions at the end of the session, this description of therapist and client "exploring differences that have already happened" was most frequently seen in the second session or later. But the focus on searching for exceptions has forced us to move that description into the early part of the first session (Gingerich, de Shazer, and Weiner-Davis, 1987).

We can now describe the process in this way: From the beginning of the first session, the therapist and client are constructing a therapeutic reality based on *continuing* transformation or change (as evidenced by any exceptions), rather than on *initiating* change. When exceptions are identified, the homework task will usually include the idea that the client should do more of what they are already doing rather than suggesting that they do something new.

FOCUSING ON SOLUTION

The Miracle Question

> *"Suppose that one night, while you were asleep, there was a miracle and this problem was solved. How would you know? What would be different? How will your husband know without your saying a word to him about it?"*

A framework for a whole series of questions (known collectively as "the miracle question") is used in almost every first session at BFTC to help client and therapist alike to describe what a solution will look like. Typically, when directly asked about their goals for therapy, clients will talk about wanting to "feel better" or wanting to have "better communication" or something equally global and non-specific. Indirectly asking about goals, using the miracle sequence, consistently elicits descriptions of concrete and specific behaviors. We have found this way of quickly looking into the future to be a most effective frame for helping clients set goals and thus describe how they will know when the problem is solved. Perhaps, as Weakland (1987) put it, this framework taps into clients' expectations for therapy: they come to therapy wanting a miracle.

Through the use of the miracle question, the therapist and client are able to have as clear a picture as possible of what a solution will look like even when the problem is vague, confused, or otherwise poorly described.

A description of the future without the complaint can be useful in assessing the salience of exceptions. When the description of the future includes a continuance of the exception (i.e., more dry beds), then we can be more sure we are on the right track. If, however, the responses to the miracle sequence are not based on the exceptions (i.e., going to school on time and getting good grades), then we know we need to redefine the complaint (i.e., the complaint is broader that "just wet beds" and includes child's misbehavior around school and therefore occasional dry beds may not be an exception to the more general complaint; The therapist then needs to continue searching for viable exceptions to the broader complaint).

SOLUTION ALWAYS COMES BEFORE PROBLEM

Historically psychotherapy has concerned itself with problems (variously defined) and solutions (seldom defined at all), with the problems receiving the major share of the effort. In fact, solutions have been looked at so rarely that solution has become the hidden half of the "problem/solution" distinction. This has led to a muddle because the distinction marker or the slash has become a barrier and the distinction itself has become a dichotomy. Psychotherapy has always mentioned goals; sometimes in terms of utopian, complete cures, other times in terms of personality reconstruction, and yet other times in terms of behavior modification. But, throughout the years, the concentration of therapeutic thought, study, and research has been on problems. Thus psychotherapy has developed a blind spot toward the realization that a concept of solution must be developed before there can even be a concept called "problem." "Problem" is just one of the many ways such events can be labeled and understood. It is a gestalt with solution being the ground to the figure of the problem. Without the idea that problems can be solved, what are called problems in the psychotherapy world would become just "facts-of-life" or unfortunate occurrences which could not be avoided and/or changed.

Our work at BFTC may seem to have just reversed the process by looking exclusively at the solution side of the distinction. At first glance we seem to be creating a new dichotomy out of the distinction. However, this view is misguided. Most simply stated, problems are problems and they can best be understood in relation to their solutions.

For example, when a solution develops out of a structural view of the problem, then the structural view proved itself useful. This does not, however, prove or disprove the structural view: it just demonstrates usefulness in that particular case or cases. Fish and Piercy (1987) describe structural therapy as

> based on the theoretical assumption that families are evolving, hierarchical organizations, with rules, or transactional patterns, for interacting across and within subsystems ... symptomatic behavior is maintained by an inadequate hierarchy and boundaries, and improving a family's organization will change not only the symptomatic behavior, but the individuals who are a part of that organization (p. 122).

On the other hand, they describe strategic therapy as

> based on the theoretical assumption that behavior, which occurs as a part of a sequence of ongoing interactional recursive events, can only be understood in context. Symptoms are embedded in these sequences of interaction, and are developed and main-

tained by ineffective solutions. [Symptoms are not inherently problematic] but rather, are construed as such, based on the reality created by the family. Therapy aims to change this reality (p. 123).

Although the words are strikingly different, on one level of abstraction the two schools of thought are saying much the same thing: problems can be seen to maintain themselves because of the context in which they happen. As Sluzki (1983) put it, this

> leads to the inescapable conclusion that symptomatic/problematic behaviors can be said to be contained and anchored by their own participation in circular, self-perpetuating patterns, by their function as reinforcers and reminders of structural traits, which recursively contribute to maintain them, and by their participation in world views that in turn provide the ideology that supports them (p. 474).

Although social learning theory and psychodynamic theory (Feldman and Pinsof, 1982) conceptualize what is going on in disparate ways, nonetheless they too focus on problem maintenance. Regardless of "how" problems are maintained and how many different views there are about this, a general statement can be made: problems are problems because they are maintained. Problems are held together simply by their being described as "problems."

If I were to observe a structural therapist and her client working together throughout the course of a case, I might punctuate the sequence of events in a very different way. Perhaps I would see the solution develop in response to the mother's doing something different in response to her daughter's problematic behavior. This follows a general law about solutions involving someone doing something different. For a structural therapist it would be very appropriate that mother was the one to do something different because it relates to her idea of hierarchy. For me this solution does not have anything whatsoever to do with the hierarchy; it is simply that someone did something different that led to a solution. Therefore, with a similar case I might simply use one of our formula tasks: Do something different. Anyone – mother, father, son, or daughter – might do something different that would lead to a solution. If it was just mother in the office, then mother might be given that task. Or daughter. Or father. Or the daughter's boyfriend. This more general view, developed by looking at solutions, removes some of the constraints that are built into structural and other views.

The next step is to look at what the therapist did that was useful in prompting mother to do something different. If she had been working on helping mother and daughter draw more appropriate boundaries or to realign the hierarchy, then mother's new behavior shows the usefulness of her approach in prompting something different to happen. It does not, however, prove the structural view or the concepts of hierarchy and boundary. It only shows that the structural approach can be useful.

That is, any view of the problematic situation might prove effective if it leads the therapist to do something useful toward prompting someone's doing something different. None of the various views are wrong and none are right. In general, solutions simply involve someone's doing something different or seeing something differently which leads to an increase in satisfaction. This more general view of solution and problem has lead BFTC to a simplified approach that has fewer constraints in defining how a solution can be achieved.

CONCLUSION

Since the therapist has focused right from the start of the session on what the client was already doing that works, *cooperation* (de Shazer, 1982b, 1985) is readily developed and promoted. The therapeutic task, when constructed in this way, allows the therapist to readily develop an intervention that *fits* (de Shazer, 1985) since the intervention just asks the client to continue to do something. This process of solution development can be summed up as helping an unrecognized difference become a difference that makes a difference.

People often find it difficult to stop trying to solve a problem because "down deep" they (we) stick to thinking that an explanation is both realizable and indispensable if a problem is to be really resolved. Solutions to problems are frequently missed because they often look like mere preliminaries; we end up searching for explanations believing that without explanation a solution is irrational, not recognizing that the solution itself is its own best explanation.

2

DISCIPLINED OBSERVATION

At first glance, the therapeutic interview seems designed to gather information. Most likely from the clients' perspective, the therapist is after nothing but the facts about the problem (i.e., a medical diagnosis is only about the facts of the symptom). In fact, many therapists refer to what they do as "problem solving."

This can certainly be a valid and useful outlook as long as therapists keep in mind that these "problems" happen or occur *outside* of the therapeutic relationship or setting. The therapist never actually deals with "problems," rather she deals with her clients' reports or depictions of the "problems" (Miller, 1986). The problems themselves include various aspects which the clients can describe: thoughts, feelings, situations, perceptions, and behaviors, all of which occur in a context that is not the therapy setting.

Of course therapists and clients act "as if" doing therapy or talking about change is separate from the changes that it helps to produce. Changes are seen to happen in the clients' "real life" outside the therapy situation. Whatever the clients report, the therapist takes it at face value. That is, for the therapist reported change is "change," and the relevance of talking about change in the future is only born out by the clients, in subsequent sessions, actually reporting changes.

Calling something a "problem" is only one of many ways that people may use to make sense of what happens in their lives. Whether or not an event is "a problem" needing therapy is dependent on how the participants construct their experience. When clients come to therapy, they report on these problematic thoughts, feelings, perceptions, situations, behaviors, and contexts within a different context, the therapeutic situation. Real life problems are the territory clients deal with while therapists only deal with maps of that territory, i.e., clients' depictions. However, they work together "as if" changing the map represents changing the territory. This distinction needs to be kept clear otherwise muddles develop when maps become confused with the territory they represent.

The interview involves an interactional process that encompasses at least two people with two different roles — therapist and client. It is not so simple a procedure that the clients simply report on how they construct the problematic aspects of life. What the therapist chooses to ask about or to comment on helps to determine how clients construct their experiences and therefore what they report and how they report on it. As Deissler (1986) suggests, therapist and client co-construct the therapeutic interview and thus they are co-authors of their shared reality.

Although the decision about what kind of intervention to use can be seen as based on the results of accumulating certain kinds of descriptions (i.e., whether an exception is spontaneous or deliberate, etc.) during the course of an interview, this may be an illusion brought about by the form of the description itself. When looked at this way, a decision tree seems implied that takes the form "If this, then that; if that, then this," etc.

The actual sequence of events during the session may be more for the client's sake than it is for the purposes of intervention and task design. The logical progression of the conversation during the session may be primarily useful for making the therapeutic intervention seem reasonable to the client.

AN ALTERNATIVE VIEW

The transferability of tasks from case to case, from client to client, some of which do not depend on the complaint or the form that the interview takes, suggests a different kind of decision tree, one based on a different iterative process: "If this, then not that." That is, it is easy to imagine that an experienced therapist has a file with ALL KNOWN TASKS[1] available to him. Each question and answer, each sequence of the conversation, the type of relationship that is developing, etc. all help the therapist to decide what *not* to do and which tasks to *not* use.

For instance, when a client presents herself as really wanting to do something about her complaint, this eliminates certain options: not giving a task or giving a purely observational task. Furthermore, if she describes an ongoing exception, then all tasks aimed at stopping something are eliminated. If her confidence is high about her ability to continue the exceptional behaviors, then tasks with random aspects are discarded and so are prediction tasks. Looked at in this way, by the time the therapist leaves the room to consult or think about the case, many or even most of the ALL KNOWN TASKS have been eliminated and the choice is narrowed down to only a few remaining possibilities.

WHAT, EXACTLY, DO BRIEF THERAPISTS DO?

A conversation between two people, even a therapeutic interview, is very loose in organization and, unless looked at in a specified way, is likely to appear tangled. It can even seem that we have a jigsaw puzzle with some wrong pieces or not enough pieces or too many. However, all the necessary pieces are there. All the observer has to do is look at them carefully and arrange them. Without disciplined observation, looking at a therapy session is like looking through a microscope for the first time. Since you do not know what you are looking at, all you see are worms, bubbles, and hair. But once you know what to look for and your observation is disciplined, then what you see makes sense.

---

[1]An ALL KNOWN TASKS file can be abstracted from: de Shazer, 1982a, 1985; Fisch, Weakland, and Segal, 1983; Haley, 1963, 1967, 1976, and from simply observing what works.

BRIEFER I

SESSION A

1. Has someone already started doing something? Is there a DELIB-ERATE exception?
Yes
2. Do they know what they need to do to keep these behaviors, involved in the exception, going?
Yes
3. Are they confident about keeping it going?
No
4. Was the miracle question used?
Yes
5. Was the response consistent with the exceptions?
Yes

SESSION B

1. Has someone already started doing something? Is there a DELIB-ERATE exception?
No
2. Are there spontaneous exceptions to the problem pattern or to the perception of the problem pattern?
No
3. Can the client imagine a solution ("miracle question")?
No
4. Do you [the therapist] think there is a realistic solution?
Yes

The above exchanges between a "expert system" asking the questions and a therapist answering them include the sort of questions and answers that a therapist working within this theory of solution would ask himself or that a consultant or the team behind the mirror might ask to help them organize their observations of a session. This expert system is a computer program designed to assist in formulating a task in the first session (de Shazer, Gingerich, Goodman, 1987; Goodman, 1986; Goodman, Gingerich, and de Shazer,

1987; Kim, de Shazer, Gingerich, and Kim, 1987). Generally speaking, expert systems are computer programs that are built on the expertise of a human expert in order to consult on a specific problem. As such, they are rule based and the steps the program uses are highly predictable. The idea behind this expert system is to make the knowledge of the team at BFTC more communicable and explicit.

From the "yes" and "no" answers to the same first question in each sequence we can see that the two sessions are being constructed differently and will therefore evolve differently. Predictably, the two sessions will *not* result in the therapist giving the same task: In case A a deliberate exception was described which can be built on while in case B no exception has been described.

The successful or unsuccessful search for exceptions is a central point of the theory of solution; here our descriptions of cases divide into major groups. Logically and predictably, another case that followed the same path A up to this point should lead the therapist to picking a task from the same class of tasks. In both of these similar cases, any task that is given should be quite different from a task given following pathway B. Otherwise, there is little or no significance to the theory.

Theory construction demands that the resulting map have a high degree of rigor. It is not enough that one step *logically* follows another: these steps need to follow each other *predictably*. Most work of this kind has been done in a laboratory where the behavior of all parties is highly constrained and manipulated (see, for instance, Berger, Fisek, Norman, and Zelditch, 1977). However, the therapy situation is comparatively unconstrained, which makes for difficulty in constructing a theory of this type, specifying what exactly a therapist does.

To avoid confusion and muddle, it is necessary to be clear about expert systems. They started off as a branch of "Artificial Intelligence," using the same computer programming language: LISP (for instance, see: Winston and Horn, 1984). The label, "Artificial Intelligence," suggests that programs or computers might actually "think." But expert systems, at least, are not the embodiment of the fabled "thinking machine." All they are capable of doing is rigorously following the rules in the program.[2]

The illusion of thinking is provoked because a program written in LISP seems to learn as it goes along. If the user activates one rule (with a specific consequence: the "then" part) at a particular time [rule 110 below] and subsequently activates another rule (with a different consequence) [rule 113 below], the result may be a modification of the first rule's consequence. But this does not mean that it thinks; it only follows "if-then" rules where the "then" of one rule becomes the "if" of another rule. Thus a program may call upon a good many rules that interact with each other before a conclusion is reached.

What follows are BRIEFER I's rules concerning situations in which the therapist is able to help the client describe an exception that involves a deliberate change in the client's behavior.

RULES

(Rule 110
  (If (there is a deliberate exception)
    (they are clear about what they need to keep doing)
    (they are confident that they can keep it going))
  (Then (give task to do more of what they are doing)))[3]
(Rule 111
  (If (there is a deliberate exception)

---

[2]Despite what Luddites think, neither God nor Beelzebub live behind the computer's screen. Computers are just machines that rigidly follow the programmer's rules. (Do stupid rules=Artificial Stupidity?)
[3]An actual Rule from BRIEFER I, written in LISP:
(patom "Has someone already started doing something? – i.e. – is there a DELIBERATE exception") (terpri) (terpri)
(setq response (read))
(cond[(equal response 'y)
    (setq assertions (cons (there is a deliberate exception) assertions)) (go four-A)]

(response to miracle question is consistent with what they are
doing)))
(Then (give a task to do more of what they are doing)))
(Rule 113
(If (there is a deliberate exception)
(they are not confident that they can keep it going))
(Then (give task to notice what is different about those occasions
when they keep change going)))

The first rule (110) states that "if there is a deliberate
exception," *and* the client is clear about the behaviors involved, *and* the client is confident that they can perform
those behaviors, *then* the therapist should simply suggest
that the client continue to perform those behaviors. This
idea is reinforced because the client's response to the miracle
question (rule 111) was consistent with the exceptions, i.e.,
the same behaviors that were involved in the exceptions are
seen as part of the solution. (If the response to the miracle
question had been inconsistent [i.e., it had little or nothing
to do with the exceptional behaviors], then different advice
would be appropriate because the client does not see the
exception, although effective, as relevant to the solution.)
Additionally, the therapist thinks that the client is not confident (rule 113) about being able to continue to perform those
behaviors (which in effect modifies rule 110) and thus the
expert system suggests a more conservative approach, i.e.,
the therapist is advised to suggest that the client pay attention to what is going on when he is able to perform the exceptional behaviors. (If the therapist had thought the client was
confident, then the simple suggestion of "do more of what is
working" (rule 110) would be the advice of the expert system.)
Of course this is not all there is to intervention design or

[(equal response 'n)
(setq assertions (cons (there is no deliberate exception) assertions)) (go
five)]

[(equal response 'x) (go five)]

selection and this is not the whole of the program. This sample only describes a brief segment dealing exclusively with deliberate exceptions. Other segments deal with spontaneous exceptions and cases where exceptions have not been described. Each of the rules interacts with various other rules and each of the segments (or clusters of rules) can be drawn as decision trees or branches of a larger decision tree. There are clusters of rules for each of the decisions on the graph of the theory or the CENTRAL MAP (see chapter 6), i.e., rules about exceptions of both kinds, hypothetical solutions, vaguely described complaints, confidence, etc.

Although the majority of the rules concern the form or pattern of the interview (i.e., questions about exceptions, etc.), other rules deal with other considerations:

GENERAL QUESTIONS BASED ON GENERAL RULES OF THUMB

Does the problem concern:
  (a) parent and child
  (b) couple
  (c) individual
  (d) individual and absent other
  (e) other
Was the therapist able to get the client to follow nonverbal leads?
Are other individuals contributing to the problem?
Is there too much information?
Was the ratio of problem talk to solution talk high?
  Did the therapist have difficulty directing problem talk into solution talk?
Did the couple leave an empty chair between them?

For instance, if the couple did leave an empty chair between them, then the user is advised to address any task to them as individuals rather than as a unit. If the user thinks there is "too much information," then he is advised to invite fewer people to the next session.[4]

---

[4]Having too many people is not the "cause" of too much information, but having fewer people will allow the therapist to reorganize his or her observations more easily.

The expert system, built to advise on the design of therapeutic interventions, has been used to help us discipline our observations. The rules the therapists (at BFTC) follow in designing interventions have been written into the program, leading to a highly rigorous theoretical map built on predictability rather than on logic and heuristic rules of thumb. The program has been used as a technical language or method with which to discipline imagination, observation, and even logic. Simply, the theory (expressed as a map in Chapter 6) is expressed as a computer program in the expert system form.

This expert system has been used as a research tool for the theory construction project. It has been used to "match" the rules with a number of cases looking for both confirmation and disconfirmation of the system's usefulness (and, therefore, the theory's usefulness). It is both the result of disciplined observation and a tool for disciplining observation. To design and built an expert system, the programmer spends many hours talking with his experts, sometimes asking naive questions, all meant to extract their observations in a coherent manner. (The domain is called "knowledge engineering" and the conversations with the experts are called "mining.")

CASE EXAMPLE ONE: A COMPLETE SESSION

Without direct observation either live or with videotape, imagining how a therapist implements the theory behind his or her work is often very difficult and misunderstanding frequently develops. A transcript of a therapy session is as close to direct observation as the printed word allows. So, in order to begin the process of constructing a theory of solution, a transcript of an interview will provide the raw material.

To illustrate, a transcript of an initial therapy session follows. This is intertwined with a transcript of a cconsulting session with the expert system on this case. Interspersed with both is a minimum of explanatory comments. The program's advice and the rules this is based on are followed by the actual intervention message to the client.

Prior to meeting the client, I only knew her name, address, phone number, and that she thought she had to come in to see me immediately. This is standard procedure at BFTC designed to minimize therapist bias. (A group of trainees was behind the mirror.)

Therapist: You thought you had to come in today and therefore what I want to know is, how you're going to know that coming in today was worth it to you. What do you have to get out of today, so that you know it's worth it to you?

Client: I have to make some decisions and to make some plans for my future course in life.

T: Today?

C: Well, I thought it was important to come up with some ideas anyway, instead of just living in complete chaos.

T: OK.

C: So at least to get a direction of some sort, even if it's temporary.

T: What decisions do you need to make today?

C: Well, I need to make . . . I'm separated from my husband, and my husband was having an affair. He may still be having an affair. My husband wants to reconcile with me, but I don't think he's too sure that he wants to give up this other person, or what he wants to do.

T: Of course you want him to give her up?

C: Um hmm, so I asked him to do that and he said that, that was something he had to decide and if he did it just because I wanted him to do it, it would cause further problems down the line.

T: So, you've been waiting around for him to make that decision?

C: Well, I guess I don't know what to do now . . . I've

T: (Interrupting) But, what're your choices as you see it?

C: My choice is doing nothing and wait for him.

T: How long is that what you've been doing?

C: It's just a couple of weeks.

T: What's your other choice?

C: To go on with my life and eliminate him from my life. Or

to go on with my life with him in the picture, but not dominating the picture. Any more? I think that's all.

T: (Inaudible) if going on with your life means without him?

C: Without him, yeah . . . that's where I can't quite understand what to do because it's hard for me to care about him and yet be put in this predicament. I wonder if it isn't easier to just try and not care about him at all, not try to look towards the future with him in any way or to try and take it as it comes and, at the same time, build some kind of life for myself.

T: How interested are you in him?

C: Oh, that changes all the time.

T: OK. Today? How pissed are you at him?

C: Not real much. I wasn't, I was fine. But, what he's doing is, he will come to me and say "Let's go out and do something really fun. I love you. I'll never see this other person again. We're going to start building our lives together." We go out. Two days later, he'll call me and he'll tell me "Well, I'm not too sure if I still want to see her." And he does this to me every three days.

T: And, at that point, you hit the top of the pissed scale?

C: Right. The other times, I'm torn between believing him, not believing him. Ummm, he says things like, "Well, If you go out, that will just alienate me." You know? Or then he'll say, two days later, "Well, why don't you go out?" You know. He means that in a very . . . he doesn't mean "go out on a date," or something like that. He means "go shopping," or "out to dinner with a girlfriend." I think he wants —

T: (Interrupting) his cake and eat it too.

C: That's what he wants, exactly.

T: That's not very fair.

C: No.

Consulting BRIEFER I, Part 1

This program is designed to assist in formulating a task for the first session. Please answer the following questions with a y for yes, an n for no and an x for undecided or does not apply. When more formal

replies are requested please be brief and do not punctuate. Thanks
for taking time to consult BRIEFER. We hope the advice will be
helpful.

What is the name of the case?
Decisions
**What does the therapist think the problem is? Write vague if neces-
sary.**
How to respond to unfaithful husband.
Would the client agree that this is the problem?
Yes

Please respond with an a,b,c etc. to the following question.
   Does the problem concern:
      (a) parent and child
      (b) couple
      (c) individual
      (d) individual and absent-party
      (e) other

Answer "c" was picked because the client is complaining
about how she is responding and she says that is what she
wants to change. If she were complaining about her husband and wanting to change him, then the response would
have been "d." The same thinking went into deciding how
best to describe the complaint.

T: On the other days, if you're not at the top of this scale,
    where are you the rest of the time?
C: Sick. Not even angry.
T: How come?
C: I once felt angry. As soon as I found out about this, I
    went through about two weeks of complete hatred.
T: Sure.
C: Until I was so filled with hatred that it was like, I said I
    can't take hatred anymore. I just can't live my life feel-
    ing this terrible hatred. I was just miserable. *So, it was
    better to be just kind of nothing.*

The italic statement might be a clue that she is going to
start describing an exception: She made a decision about

how to handle her response. I began to explore its potential usefulness.

T: So, you decided on nothing? That's good. OK, that sounds like a wise choice. How easy is it then?

C: Hard.

T: Yeah. (Long pause) How hard?

C: You mean to be nothing?

T: Yes.

C: Well, it's not really nothing because there's a lot of hurt involved that doesn't express through anger. It's just hurt.

T: And, that's easier on you than the hatred.

C: More so than with hatred and hurt at the same time as before. I mean, it's just there so it's just a matter of what else to do with it.

This seemed to be a dead-end, so I returned to clarifying the complaint and searching for exceptions.

T: So, the choice as I understand it then is go it alone from day-to-day, and sort of exclude him from whatever's left down that trail?

C: Um hmm.

T: So, that's trail one: going it alone. OK. Trail two is essentially to keep doing what you're doing –

C: (Interrupting) No.

T: just waiting for him to make up his mind.

C: (Interrupting) No, that would be more like, I'll go out and do what I want to do and when I want to see him, I'll see him. When I don't want to see him, I won't see him. But he wants control of my choice.

T: That's go it alone, but leave room for him. OK, and the third trail is continuing doing what you're doing.

C: Right.

T: OK. Which I guess, since you're here today, means that it hasn't been working for you.

C: No, I can't do it that way.

The potential exception has unexpectedly turned out to be part of the complaint. The search continues.

T: OK, so we can cross that one out. Is there a fourth alternative?
C: Go back together with him.
T: On his terms or your terms?
C: I don't know.
T: Back together means that he's got rid of her?
C: Yes.
T: OK, your terms. Is there a fifth one? Well, let's take a look at the fourth one. He says he doesn't know (inaudible) on this girlfriend business, so . . .
C: But he says it isn't because of the girlfriend, he says that it's because of me. Since I found out that he had this affair, that I've changed.
T: Of course.
C: So he thinks, that if he wasn't –
T: (Interrupting) You weren't supposed to change?
C: He thinks I'll change back. *He thinks I'm nicer since he did this and that if he . . . I don't know, he thinks that if he gets rid of her, then I'll change back to "not nice," then he'll have nobody.*

The italic text may be a potential exception that is worth exploring.

T: Oh sure, OK –
C: (Interrupting) So that's his point.
T: I see. Do you agree? Have you been nicer?
C: I've changed . . . I have changed in some ways, that's true.
T: "Nicer"?
C: To some degree.
T: Then, from his point of view, maybe he ought to keep her until you're perfectly nice?
C: Well, he knows that that isn't going to continue. My

"nice" right now is at its brink, I mean it isn't going to
continue.

T: You think that it isn't working for you?

C: No.

Another potential exception has turned into yet another
aspect of the complaint.

T: OK. So, how is he going to know you're "nice enough" to
   get rid of her?

C: I don't know. That's his dilemma.

T: Um hmm. What's he doing about it?

C: Well, he says that he isn't seeing her, but that he doesn't
   trust me! And, what's so crazy is, he doesn't trust me
   and he's the one who had the affair. And I'm thinking,
   this is crazy. How can he not trust me, when, you
   know . . .

T: Maybe he thinks that if he has the right to do that, then
   so do you.

C: If he has the right to do?

T: An affair, so do you.

C: You mean he wants me to have an affair?

T: No, no, no, that's what he is afraid of.

C: He wouldn't want that at all!

T: OK. So, getting back together now doesn't seem viable. Is
   there any fifth one? (Long pause.) Well, we'll think of
   one. There probably is, there usually is.

Pragmatically, difficulty making a decision is usually due
to the person's not finding any alternative to be more positive than the rest. Therefore, an "empty alternative," one
that is not specified, leaves room for both creativity and
chance.

T: OK, So, if you're saying that what you've been doing isn't
   working for you so you want to stop that. At this point
   we can see that there are three or four or five possible
   trails you could take. One is to go it alone, put him aside,

go on with your life. Two is to go it alone, leaving room
for him to do his own thing and get things rolling again.
Three is to work at it somehow – getting back together.
Four is . . .

C: Um hmm.

T: OK.

C: He thinks the second and third are the same.

T: How so?

C: Because, he thinks that I . . . He hasn't said to me that he
isn't going to go out, or that if we get back together that
he wouldn't go out. Not not go out with this person, but
just go out drinking until three in the morning or whatever –

T: (Interrupting) That's something he did?

C: Well yeah. Well, I don't know, maybe that's not what he
was doing at the time. I just know what he wasn't doing,
but he thinks that he wants me to go out, but he doesn't
want me to do what he's doing.

T: Right. Well, the main decision, which trail to take? What
difference is that going to make?

At this point, I decided to begin looking for how she will
know when the problem is solved. In this way, perhaps, we
can find a usable exception or a hypothetical solution to
build on.

C: It makes me feel organized. I'm going in a direction. Like,
I'm more in control of what I'm doing, deciding. Not
being told, or manipulated or anything. It's deciding
that this is what I want to do and you do what you want
to do. I haven't been able to do that.

T: Let's take the first trail. Go it alone. And, six months
from now, having made that decision, six months from
now, what do you see going that route?

C: (Long pause.) Structure. . . .

T: What else do you see?

C: I just think that my life would fall into a pattern of some
sort, not necessarily that I would be happy, but that my

life will be planned. I would know what I was doing a lot, because I wouldn't have another person interfering with my plans. Therefore, I'd be totally in control of my situation. I would control it, I would plan it and organize it and —

T: (Interrupting. Inaudible). OK, and taking the other trail over here is, going it alone, but leaving room for him. Six months from now, what do you see there? How different is it?

C: It affects my decision making. I lose control of the situation.

T: OK. So, going it alone, but leaving room for him, gives you less control.

C: Right.

T: OK and, getting back together, six months from now, what then?

C: (Long pause.) I don't know. I don't know if anything can be rebuilt. I don't know, I couldn't live through what I went through before . . . that was (inaudible) realistically. I would like to do that, but I don't even know if that's a possibility. I don't know, there's so much that would have to happen to make that situation work.

T: Starting with his throwing her out entirely of his life.

C: Certainly.

T: That's the first thing that has to happen on that trail. OK, until he does that, that trail is purely hypothetical.

C: Right.

T: And he doesn't seem inclined to do that right now.

C: He said he won't see her, but he kind of leaves it open, like well, "I might run into her."

T: Promises aren't worth the paper they're written on. So, until you are convinced he is going to throw her out, she's still there.

C: She's still left in the situation, no doubt about that.

T: The only route that looks fairly decent, so far, is going it alone. With things under your control. The rest of the options are no different from what you've got right now and that you don't like.

C: (Long pause.) That's true. The second option would be different if I could desensitize myself. It would be like living a double life, but I don't know if I can do that.

T: That certainly makes things, less control, if you will. Keeping as much control as you can — feasibly possible. We all know about bad luck and good luck, accidents of one sort or another (inaudible). There's only as much control as you can reasonably expect. The third option is beyond your control.

C: Yes.

T: I mean, he's got to start it.

C: Right.

T: So, the choice between one and two. Where do you have room for him? What good would it do?

C: (Long pause.) Well, I guess it would be easier in that he's part of my life. I wouldn't be completely ignored. I mean, I wouldn't be quite, starting over quite from scratch.

T: I see . . . your feeling that he is part of your life somehow, how important is that?

C: It is and I don't understand that! I think that's crazy and I think that's crazy that I think that.

T: You've been married how many years?

C: Ten.

T: It's habit, if nothing else, that makes him part of your life.

C: (Interrupting) True.

T: But, how important is he? How important is it that he's part of your life?

C: I don't know if that's more important than tranquility. That's what I'm trying to weigh. I don't know which end would really be tranquil or how it would work —

T: (Interrupting) Right. As long as you're doing what's good for you.

C: Does it?

T: That the way it works.

C: Hmmm.

T: Just decide, what's good for you. So far it looks like one is good for you. Two we're still playing with yet, right? I don't know if it's good for you. OK, what good would it do you to leave room for him in your life?

C: I wouldn't be alone, and I seem to have an intangible need to be with him, but it's a hurtful type of need.

T: I'm still a little confused about that.

C: (Laughing) I am too.

T: OK. Well, let's put it this way. Let's say, three months from now, watching you on a hidden camera, how would any one know whether you picked one over two? What difference would it make? Or you picked two over one? What difference would it make?

C: Because, with two I'd end up with him again, and one I wouldn't.

T: Right. How important is that? Back to that question!

C: I don't know if it's possible for things to change. I don't know if it's possible for me to trust.

T: So, its a gamble.

C: Yeah, it's a gamble.

T: How big of a risk is it?

C: I will take that risk if I thought I wouldn't lose my sanity in the process.

She is really caught on the **either/or** of her construction, i.e., **either** be in control **or** be under control and **either** be alone **or** be with him. A reconstruction might be designed around substituting a **both/and** construction.

T: I think I've got that. How can you do that?

C: Well, if instead of having such a, just being able to develop a nonchalant type of relationship instead of such an intense relationship.

T: How good are you at pretending?

C: Not good.

T: Good enough to fool him?

C: Yes.

T: OK. so it is possible for you to have your cake and eat it too . . . That is, you could go it alone, pretending to leave room for him, in case he changes.

C: Um, yeah.

T: Meanwhile making plans like he's not part of your life.

C: Right.

T: If you combine the two —

C: (Interrupting) Right.

T: Pretend, just enough, so that he thinks you're leaving room for him and, if he changes — then you change your plans. Does that make sense?

C: Yes.

T: And, you can do that.

C: I'd like to be able to do that.

T: What's it going to take?

C: More self-confidence.

T: Where are you going to buy that? Where does that come from?

C: Just making myself do things.

T: How good are you at that? You know how to do that.

C: Yes.

T: What else do you need to do?

C: I don't know.

T: Supposing he was sitting over there, and we asked him. What would he say?

C: Be with him.

T: OK. And, you want to do that. Now, in order to be with him and make it good for you, what do you have to do?

C: I have to detach from him, because if I don't, it won't work.

T: Right.

C: He would just have to be another person, like any other person I would be seeing.

T: OK.

C: And, that is, I wouldn't have to, I would not have expectations of him.

T: So, if he —

C: (Interrupting) I've covered myself.

T: Right. So, if he calls up and says, "Let's go to the Bucks game" and you'd say, "I'm sorry I've got other plans."

C: Um hmmm.

T: Keeping your distance. Or, you could call him up and ask him out if you felt like it.

C: The thing is, there's a risk, although I don't think he will, he could go back to his girlfriend.

T: And you don't want that.

C: Right.

T: What else do you need to do to convince him that there's room? What else do you need to do?

C: Cooperate with him —

T: (Interrupting) Like what?

C: *Not getting angry, that would be tops. Not getting angry over things and telling him he's a jerk.*

T: So, did you tell him that before you separated?

C: All the time.

T: That's part of being nice, not telling him he's a jerk?

C: Right.

In this context, not telling him that he is a jerk may prove to be a useful exception.

T: So, how are you going to do that? How are you going to keep yourself from falling back into the old pattern of calling him a jerk when he's a jerk?

C: If I'm detached from him, I wouldn't do that.

T: Right.

C: Whether he's a jerk or not, it doesn't matter.

T: How difficult will it be not to call him a jerk when he's a jerk?

C: *I don't know, I've been doing that for the last few weeks and it seems to work.*

Here is an useful exception that she can build on, one that can — potentially — make a difference to her and to them.

T: OK, so that part of being "nice" you want to keep.

C: Yes.

T: OK. Is there anything else you want to deal with today before I go talk to the team?

C: Yeah, one question is that I don't know, see he's going to ask me about this, what I'm doing. And I don't know if I should tell him what I'm doing or just not anything.

T: What difference would it make, are you thinking?

C: He'll nag me and nag me. I'm not used to my life being separate from his life, so I don't know how much to share and how much not to share.

T: OK. Why don't you think about that while I go talk to the team and then I'll be back in five or ten minutes, something like that.

C: OK.

Consulting BRIEFER I, PART 2

Has someone already started doing something?—i.e.—is there a DELIBERATE exception?
No
Are there SPONTANEOUS exceptions to the problem pattern or to the perception of the problem pattern?
Yes

Once an exception is identified, the program sets about asking more questions about the nature of the exception.

Can the exceptions be defined in behavioral terms?
Yes
Has the exception occurred recently?
Yes
Was the exception a solution to a different problem?
No
Do the exceptions appear to be random occurrences?
Yes
Are they clear about what they need to do to make it happen again?
No
Are they confident that they can make it happen again?
No
Was the miracle question used?
No

Other questions were, however, used to both attempt to set goals and to construct how we will know when the problem is solved. This is, however, about the specific question.

The program then moves on to some general questions, aimed primarily at the kind of client-therapist relationship that is developing.

The program's structure is mapped as a flowchart that illustrates what is considered after any "yes" or "no" response from the therapist. For instance, if there were no presession changes and no exceptions, then the program will ask questions about hypothetical solutions. However, these questions will not be asked if there were exceptions.

Were other individuals present?
No
Was the therapist able to get the client to follow nonverbal leads?
X

This was not clear enough to answer "yes."

Did the client respond to the mirror instead of other stimuli in the room?
No

If the client had responded to the mirror, then the intervention message would be phrased as solely coming from the team.

Did the client nod head throughout the session?—demonstrating nonverbal agreement?
X
Is the client always disagreeing with the therapist?
No
Are other individuals contributing to the problem?
Yes

In this case, with this construction, the husband, by virtue of his unpredictable behavior (and the status of the

BRIEFER: A DEMONSTRATION PROTOTYPE
FLOWCHART OF KNOWLEDGE BASE

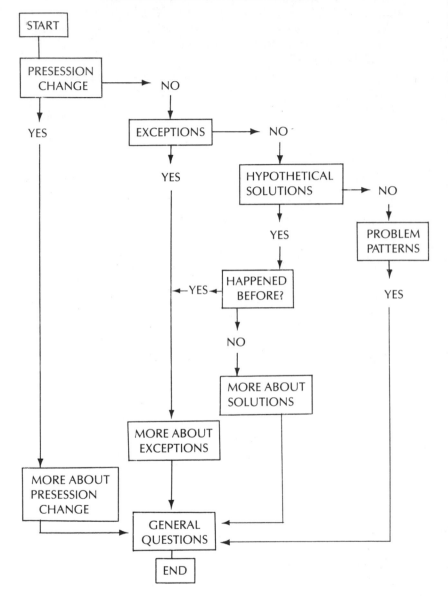

girlfriend), can be seen as contributing to her having been confused about how to handle the situation.

Is someone who seems necessary to the solution absent from this session?
No
Do you have a hunch that the client might not do a behavioral homework task?
No
Do you have a hunch that the client might not do an observational homework task?
No

At this point the program takes a little time to match the responses with the rules. When a response to a question calls up a particular rule, other rules are eliminated.

CONSULTING SESSION WITH BRIEFER I: ADVICE

Rule 200 suggests: there is a usable exception
Rule 203 suggests: include predicting or coin toss or randomness as part of the task
Rule 204 suggests: include predicting or coin toss or randomness as part of the task
Rule 212 suggests: give task to pay attention to what is going on when the exception happens
Rule 213 suggests: give task to notice what is different when exceptions do happen
Rule 589 suggests: consider giving a task that interrupts the way in which others contribute to the client's problem

If no other useful advice has been given, use the FFST.
If the same or similar advice has been given by two rules, it is strongly suggested.

Would you like to see the full text of the rules called up?
Yes

(Rule 200
  (If (there is an exception)

        (the exception can be described in behavioral terms)
        (the exception has occurred recently))
    (Then (there is a usable exception)

(Rule 203
    (If (there is an exception)
        (the exception behaviors are random occurrences))
    (Then (include predicting or coin toss or randomness as PART of the task)))

(Rule 204
    (If (there is a usable exception)
        (the exception behaviors are random occurrences))
    (Then (include predicting or coin toss or randomness as PART of the task)))

(Rule 212
    (If (there is a usable exception)
        (they are not clear about what they need to do))
    (Then (give task to pay attention to what is going on when the exception happens)))

(Rule 213
    (If (there is a usable exception)
        (they are not confident that they can do what they need to do))
    (Then (give task to notice what is different about those occasions when exceptions do happen)))

(Rule 589
    (If (individual)
        (other individuals are contributing to the problem))
    (Then (consider giving a task that interrupts the way in which others contribute to the client's problem)))

Intervention Message

T: We've certainly agreed that the direction you're going, going it alone and pretending to leave room for him seems to be the most viable option and I think and we think it's a good decision.

　　　　Now, as far as your question, which is a damn good

question by the way, we think it's pretty clear – when you stop to think about it – that, as far as he's concerned, you are as confused as ever, maybe more. You can drag that on forever or until he does something clear. That fit your thinking? Good.

(Long pause.) We think you need to act out the part in addition to saying that you're confused. For instance, when he calls and wants to do something with you, which is going to happen now and then.

C: Right.

T: You should toss a coin: HEADS=yes; TAILS=no. Even if you feel like saying "yes," but it comes up with tails, you say "no." That will give a little edge to your voice and if he says, "Why not?" your explanation could go something like this: "Well, I don't know, I'm just so confused and I just don't feel like it." Then, no more than once or twice every few weeks – something random so he can't figure out when it might come, then you give him a call. As long as you have the control over this and you decide when to make this random event happen, you give him a call and invite him out for coffee or whatever. Don't do it too often, you can feel your way with this, not very often, but not not at all. Again, if he can't figure it out at all, if he can't figure out the pattern, that's more evidence that you're still confused. You want him to think that, even though you aren't confused anymore, you want him to think that because that's the only chance you have of him shaping up and the two of you working it out. The only chance is, if he straightens it up and then comes back and initiates something with you. Otherwise, you'll have to stop pretending and go ahead and go it alone. OK, let's stop.

I don't think we need to schedule another appointment, see how it goes.

C: I feel better already.

T: Well, good luck to you.

C: Thank you. It really helped. Thanks a lot.

This intervention gives her a method to control her reactions and thus gives her some more control of her situation. She now has a way to handle him and, as a bonus, stands a chance of changing how he deals with her (since she will be more unpredictable). It also stands a chance of helping them get back together should that eventually be their decision.

INFORMAL TESTING

The program's rules proved sufficient for the case under consideration: the advice given was similar to the intervention that was actually used. Should the advice have differed from the actual intervention, then the user would need to check the input for correctness before concluding that the rules were not sufficient.

The purpose of the "test" is to find out how well the program's advice fits the facts of real cases. When the advice does not fit, then perhaps the program and its rules are insufficient for that particular case or "type of case." Revision of the rules may be simply a matter of refinement within a certain section or it may become a matter of discarding or vastly revising the program and thus the theory. Of course, revision of any theory is called for when the "facts" consistently do not fit.

This first version, called BRIEFER (Goodman, 1986; Goodman et al, 1987) was designed solely as a prototype meant only to help us figure out if it could be done at all. It was not, in any sense, designed to be complete. Further development through rule changes was fully expected. It was meant only for use with first sessions.

Results

(A) Testing the system helped to clarify the importance of the relationship between complaint description, exceptions, and goals (i.e., responses to the miracle question).

For instance, there is a considerable difference between the following complaints:

(1) The client is depressed about life in general.
(2) The client is depressed about his job.

In each case, what would be considered an exception could well be different. For instance, if the man reported that his marriage is fine, then, in version (1) that might be a viable exception, and in version (2) it probably cannot be considered an exception. Sometimes which punctuation to use is not clear and the miracle question can be useful in helping the therapist make this decision. If, in response to the miracle question, the client described a vacation with his wife, then punctuation (1) – which would consider the OK marriage as an exception – is likely to be useful. If, however, the response is built on or predicated by a different job, then punctuation (2) seems more salient.

(B) When running the program revealed a "lack of fit," the majority of time it seemed to center on the client-therapist relationship when the client group was more than one person (a couple or a family unit). In a mixed situation, the program needs to be run once for each individual. The importance of this subsequently led to a revision of the theory (i.e., it is now at the top of the map rather than in the form of general questions near the end of the consulting session).

(C) Cases done by therapists using a different approach resulted in many questions that were not answerable and, therefore, the system was unable to give useful advice. The user's inability to answer the questions suggests that the therapist he observed did not follow the model. This strongly suggests that we are actually studying what we think we are studying.

(D) The system's ability to advise on interventions taking into consideration only the pattern of the interview confirms that the theory (Chapter 6) fits within the scope conditions (Chapter 4). Only the pattern and form of the reality constructed by therapist and client need to considered for solution development.

(E) The range of cases that the expert system can handle sufficiently well suggests that the 68 rules are complex enough for those situations. The cases it does not handle well suggest that we need to continue to attempt to specify what exactly it is that the brief therapist actually does. Thus, this expression of the theory needs further development and revision.

(F) In this particular case, the advice from only six rules was called up. The second and third gave the same advice. The fourth and fifth gave similar advice. Therefore, in effect, only four rules were necessary to give the advice which was strikingly close to the actual intervention. The other pieces of advice available to BRIEFER, suggested by the remaining 62 rules were, in effect, chosen out. This seems to confirm the simplicity of the theory's specific pathways within the complexity of the whole.

(G) BRIEFER's advice is frequently very similar to that developed by the team during the consulting break. For some cases BRIEFER's advice is lengthy, because a lot of rules are called up, and, at times, this advice is contradictory. This adequately reflects the observed session and is similar to the team's discussion. The team was usually able to come to a decision about "what to do," but BRIEFER leaves the final decision up to the user.[5] Clearly, we need to specify more exactly the therapist's and team's decision-making procedures and rules in these cases.

From the start, the program was designed to assist in training therapists to use the model and the theory upon which it is based. Simply, the questions reflect the areas that are theoretically important to solution development.

BRIEFER I clearly met our expectations for a demonstration prototype. It showed that this type of knowledge could be captured by an expert system and it also showed that it held great promise as a training tool. BRIEFER I also helped us to further discipline our observation and prompted revision of our observation techniques and modifi-

---

[5] If BRIEFER were to be placed "on line," or actually used in the intervention designing process, then the "expert system" would need to be added to the scope conditions (Chapter 4).

cation of the theory's CENTRAL MAP (Chapter 6). Furthermore, experiences with BRIEFER I has led to a new expert system that is more than a major revision of BRIEFER I.

BRIEFER II

While BRIEFER I took the "if this, then that" approach, the "if this, then not that" approach has been used to build BRIEFER II (Kim, de Shazer, Gingerich, and Kim, 1987) and thus its structure is considerably different from the first. This is, in part, a result of the informal testing of BRIEFER I. The same case will be used here to illustrate the similarities and differences between the two programs. (The **bold** face print is what shows up on the computer screen.)

The first question:

Is there a complaint?
Yes

If the response is "no," then the program suggests that the therapist only give compliments since the therapist-client relationship falls within the visitor category. "Visitor" is a code word describing the therapist-client relationship when, during the interview, the therapist has been unable to help the client describe a complaint and when the therapist has been unable to help the client develop even a minimal expectation of change.

The following parameter is inferable. If you are not sure how to answer, respond by typing "nn."
Are they customers?
Y

This clearly shows the shift from the first to the second version. Here the description of the client-therapist relationship is used to divide the program into two major branches: customer and complainant.

"Complainant" is a code word describing a client-therapist relationship built on the client's having developed an expectation of change as a result of the interview. A special type of complainant is given the code word "customer," which describes a client-therapist relationship, as a result of the interview, that is built on the client's wanting to do something about building a solution.[6]

These first two responses have eliminated the suggestions: (1) Give compliments only and (2) give observation-only tasks.

> The client belongs to customer group.
> The following parameter is inferable. If you are not sure how to answer, respond by typing "nn."
> Is there an exception?
> NN
> Are there times (no matter how few) when the complaint is unexpectedly absent?
> Y
> Are these times described in behavioral terms?
> Y

This allows the program to "infer" that there is an exception and that it is viable since it is described in behavioral terms.

The responses to this point have eliminated more pathways and thus certain types of interventions. These five are all that are still under consideration.

> You may want one of the following prescriptions
>   (1) Do More
>   (2) Prediction
>   (3) Observe
>   (4) Do More + Observe
>   (5) Different Do
> The following parameter is inferable. If you are not sure how to answer, respond by typing "nn."

[6]Fisch, Weakland, and Segal (1983) use a similar distinction.

Are they confident about doing what they need to do?
NN
Do they sound confident?
N
Do they sound determined?
Y

That the therapist thinks the client sounds determined is enough for the program to infer that the client is more or less confident enough in the exception's viability and the likelihood that continuing the exception will have something to do with the solution.

Was the response to the miracle question consistent with exception(s)?
Y

This version assumes that the therapist used the specific miracle question which had not yet been developed when this session was held. However, the client's view of what things would be like when the problem is solved is clear enough and the client's goals were consistent with the exceptions, i.e., her being in control of her responses to her husband. Therefore, the question can be answered as if the miracle question had been used.

Suggestion: Give them the "Do More" Task.

Do you want to know how this prescription made?
Y
The prescription was made as follows.
  Rule 22 indicates:
    There were evidences
    The client belongs to customer group.
  Rule 80 indicates:
    There were evidences
    There is an exception to the complaint.
    The exception is described in behavioral terms.
    Those facts gave
    There is a viable exception.

Rule 100 indicates:
There were evidences
There is a viable exception.
Those facts gave
You may want one of the following prescriptions
  (1) Do more
  (2) Prediction
  (3) Observe
  (4) Do More + Observe
  (5) Different Do
Rule 51 indicates:
There were evidences
They sound determined
Those facts gave
They are confident about what they need to do.
Rule 101 indicates:
There were evidences
The client belongs to customer group.
Thank you for your cooperation, Bye!

Brief Family Therapy Center   Date: 7-28

Name: MARY
Sex: F   Age: 40

Prescription: Do more of what works

(Sample wording)
Since you found out that works for you, I can only suggest that you continue doing the same kind of thing.

Prescribed by Briefer II Expert System

A sample rule from BRIEFER II, the one that calls up the "do more of what works" task:

```
(Rule 101
  (If        (rule              r020              t)
    (rule                r100              t)
    (people           confident           t)
    (question               miracle-e                    t))
  (Then
    (treatment         task              do-more)
    (treatment         end               t)))
```

This says that:

(1) Rule 20 is true, i.e., the client is a customer.

(2) Rule 100 is true, i.e., there is a viable exception.

(3) The client is confident.

(4) The miracle question was consistent with the exception.

(5) Therefore, the "do-more" task.

(6) And finally, the questions are over. Give the end "do-more" message.

She never knows when her husband is going to contact her (i.e., it is a random complaint) and therefore, since she is going to continue to appear confused, the coin toss adds a random element to the intervention. The advice fits well enough except for not asking about the random element in the complaint. The program would need to be revised if more cases were to follow the same pathway, i.e., one that includes a random element in the complaint.

BRIEFER II is strictly work in progress and is therefore likely to change. In its current form it reflects the shift in the theory and it is thus based on an "if this, then not that" description of how brief therapists decide what to do.

Regardless of how the choice of task is made, the choice depends on how things are described rather than what things are being described. Whether the complaint be about abusing coke or making decisions, it is the form of the description of the interview that determines what kind of task is appropriate and the consulting break is used to put meat on the bones of a task.

CONCLUSION

Both BRIEFER I and BRIEFER II are frequently capable of suggesting interventions very similar to those the therapist at BFTC actually used. The majority of questions in both programs can be answered simply with "yes" and "no." This reflects the method used by the therapists at BFTC. In the main, we discipline our observations in a similar fashion, simply asking questions that call for "yes" and "no" answers. This way of disciplining observation seems to be effective in figuring out what class of intervention to use and, sometimes, which specific member of that class is more appropriate. At times BRIEFER I will not only suggest what kind of thing to do, but even suggest in part "how to do it." However, more frequently, the "how to do it," the art side of doing therapy, is strictly left up to the therapist. There is no intention to replace the therapist, rather the intent is to help therapists be disciplined in their observing and thinking.

On one level, the therapists at BFTC discipline their observations focused around the following questions which are derived from the two BRIEFERs:

(1) Is there a complaint?
Yes   No
(2) Is there an exception?
Yes   No
(3) Is there a goal?
Yes   No
(4) Is goal related to the exception's continuing?
Yes   No

The various possible sequences of answers indicate the major pathways interviews follow. This will be dealt with in detail below (see chapter 6 and the following chapters) but, for now, disciplined observation using these programs as a model has simplified the tasks of interviewing and intervention design and/or selection.

For instance, the first question clearly addresses the therapist-client relationship: if "yes" is the answer, then the relationship falls into either the "complainant" or "customer" type and therapy can begin. If during the break the therapist can answer all four questions with a "yes,'" then a class of interventions that is built around suggesting that the client do more of what works (the exception) is recommended; if the first and third are answered "yes" and the others "no," then a task oriented toward the goal is suggested, but if the answer to the first question is "no," then no task is called for because therapy has not yet begun. Of course each of the responses to these major questions is followed by more detailed questions about the pattern and form of the observed interview which are again frequently answered with "yes" and "no." Thus disciplined observation within this model calls for paying attention to how therapist and client construct the interview, and what kind of pattern the interview follows rather than focusing on what it is that is being talked about.

3

HOW TO KNOW WHAT TO DO

For therapists doing therapy with a client, a primary concern is how to know when to do what. Once that is known, a secondary concern develops: how to do what you know to do once you know when to do it? The answers to the first question come from the therapist's theory or model. What to do can be rather rigorously described in writing. Therapy, however, can be seen with imagination as well as with rigor and the answers to the second question come from less rigorous realms than the answers to the first.

Metaphorically, therapy might be seen as part art and part science and therefore might best be seen as a craft. One does not have to be a great artist to make a viable, functional ceramic pot. There are clear, teachable rules and ways to gauge failure and success. On this level, a pot is a pot. It either works, i.e., holds water, or it does not. But some pots are more than this.

We treasure pots made by the ancient Greeks and Chinese not only for their utility and antiquity: we treasure them because they are works of art. Works of art, however functional, are not measured solely by how well the maker followed the rules. Sometimes, in fact, the maker did not observe the rules that were known at the time and thus the pot is all the more precious. But, once the rule breaker has made the pot, rules for imitation and replication can be invented and other people can then make fully functional pots which follow the new rules and thus schools of pottery making come together, built around following the master's rules. Within any one school, an individual's work might stand out as art even though he or she is following the same rules as his or her peers: artists need not necessarily be revolutionary rule breakers.

In this sense, therapy is a craft. Freud and Erickson, for instance, violated the rules of their times and, as a result, can be seen as "artists" or "masters." We who come after can study their works and invent teachable rules so that our therapy, if not really art, can at least work and be functional and viable. The schools that invent rules can be seen as doing something akin to "normal science" as Kuhn (1970) used the term. "Normal scientists" plod along following rules they think and believe the paradigm's inventor himself followed and their major "problems" are found in the mysteries the master left behind.

PSEUDO-ORIENTATION IN TIME

Our work at BFTC, since 1982, has been built on solving the puzzle posed in Erickson's paper, "Pseudo-Orientation in Time as a Hypnotic Procedure" (1954), de Shazer's paper, "Brief Hypnotherapy of Two Sexual Dysfunctions: The Crystal Ball Technique" (1978a), (which was built on Erickson's paper), and the results of our experience using our Formula First Session Task (de Shazer, 1985). Erickson's

> technique was formulated by a utilization of the general appreciation that practice leads to perfection, that action once initiated tends to continue and that deeds are the offspring of hope and expectancy. These ideas are utilized to create a therapy situation in which the patient can respond effectively psychologically to desired therapeutic goals as **actualities already achieved.**
>
> This is done by employing hypnosis and using, conversely to age regression, a technique of orientation into the future. Thus the patient is enabled to

achieve a detached, dissociated, objective and yet
subjective view of what he believes at the moment
he had already accomplished, without awareness
that those accomplishments are the expression in
fantasy of his hopes and desires (in Haley, 1967, p.
369).

Although this work with crystal balls was done using
formal hypnosis, i.e., a trance induction was used, our work
at BFTC is done without any formal hypnosis. In fact, our
effort is in the opposite direction. The therapist and client
consciously and deliberately plan together what it will take
for the client to achieve a solution. It seems that in the
therapy situation, simply describing in detail a future in
which the problem is already solved helps to build the expectation that the problem will be solved and then this expectation, once formed, can help the client think and behave in
ways that will lead to fulfilling this expectation.

More important than the techniques themselves are the
ideas and assumptions that are only implicit in both crystal
ball papers (Erickson, 1954; de Shazer, 1978a), but more
explicit in BFTC's work (de Shazer, 1985; de Shazer, Berg,
Lipchik, Nunnally, Molnar, Gingerich, and Weiner-Davis,
1986). All of the therapy described in these works can be
seen as built on the assumption that the client constructs
his or her own solution based on his or her own resources
and successes. This is in sharp contrast with the more familiar therapeutic idea that there is something wrong with the
client that the therapist needs to treat and cure. In fact,
BFTC's intervention design process and interviewing proto-
col explicitly minimize talk about problems and complaints.

A careful reading of Erickson's paper might lead the con-
temporary reader to expect him to develop concrete and
highly specific tasks as interventions because he so carefully describes the clients' situations. Instead, Erickson simply
has the client, while in trance, invent his or her own solution
and then Erickson waits for the clients to return and report
on success. This is another part of the puzzle: How does

simply imagining a solution or life after the problem is resolved lead to actually solving it?

FOCUS

Most initial therapy sessions begin with the client describing the complaint or problem that led him or her to seek therapy. Frequently, the therapist will then explore the complaint in great detail, although what the therapist considers important varies from model to model. As a solution focused model has become more developed, this phase has become shorter and shorter, and has taken on less and less importance. Within a very short period of time the therapist begins constructing a solution by initiating a search for exceptions, i.e., the therapist explores in as much detail as possible times when the complaint did not happen. No matter how much the client tells the therapist about the complaint, the conversation will be brought back to when it is that the complaint does not happen. Then the therapist will switch to working with the client to describe a vision of the future when the complaint is resolved. This is done without getting a full description of the problem and/or its etiology and, surprisingly, it is sometimes done without discussing what steps might be necessary to resolve the complaint. Frequently, this vision of the solution is directly related to the exceptions continuing into the future, but sometimes not. After a brief time out, the therapist then suggests a next step toward making that constructed vision into the solution reality. In the second session the client describes whatever steps he or she had taken toward life without the complaint, a next step is defined, and the cycle repeated until the client is satisfied that a satisfactory solution has been achieved. Of course not all cases fit this description with ease, but the overall process remains the same.

Such a simple description can only be understood through a more complex explication or description. But even the one paragraph (above) suggests that this model has been influenced by the puzzle Erickson posed: solutions

need not be directly related to the problems they are meant
to solve. Of course the client's complaint needs to be resolved as part of the solution, otherwise the therapist is not
doing what the client hired him or her to do. But, to do this
successfully does not mean that the client's problem needs
to be explored in detail or defined exactly or even talked
about at great length.

HOW IS THIS POSSIBLE?

How can therapy resolve the client's complaint without
these complaints being fully understood? At BFTC the therapist might tell you that "all complaints are alike." In almost
all cases, the client's complaint includes wanting the *absence*
of something without having any idea about what a reasonable replacement might be. The client only wants to stop
being depressed, or for junior to stop wetting the bed, or to
stop arguing constantly. But, when the therapist says:
"O.K., but what will you be doing when you are no longer
depressed," or, "when junior is no longer wetting the bed," or,
"when you are no longer constantly arguing?" the client is
stumped. A frequent first response is "I (we) will be happier"
which is no doubt true, but what will the client be *doing*?
The difficulty here is that the absence of something cannot
be proved. If the depression or the arguing or the wet bed
stopped tomorrow, how can you know that it will not start
again the following day? However, if you know that jogging
every morning or random hugs or Dad's getting junior up at
7:15 every morning are part of an exception or part of an imagined solution and thus part of the goal, then you can measure
the frequency or the start of these behaviors – as they become
habitual – to see if indeed they are part of the solution. If not,
then everybody needs to do something different.

NOTHING ALWAYS HAPPENS

Simplicity does not often come about spontaneously.
Rather it evolves over a period of time and through a process that involves a lot of complicated thinking. Over the

past four years, my colleagues and I have come to realize the practical clinical importance of the folkloric idea that all "rules include exceptions." We have come to define exceptions as "whatever is happening when the complaint is not" (de Shazer, 1985, de Shazer et al, 1986).

For instance, in a case where a family complains about their son's bed wetting, we used to investigate and attempt to describe the pattern(s) involved – what was going on, what they each were doing, what happened both before and after the complaint happened. The idea was that once we knew the pattern of interaction, appropriate interventions could be designed to help the family vary that pattern and thus eliminate the wet beds. This approach works quite well but unfortunately not all complaints are described well enough for the therapist and family to know about the patterns in enough detail to effectively use this approach. In fact, in many cases the therapist is unable to help the family describe a clear pattern and the observers behind the screen are not able to abstract a pattern description from the conversation during the session even after repeatedly watching the videotape.

BUT IT CAN'T BE *THAT* SIMPLE!

A result of searching for exceptions and finding them in case after case has taught us that there are times when the complaint is absent, i.e., when the bed is dry. That is, at some times and in some contexts, the boy *knows how* to have a dry bed. A terribly simple idea! Given all our previous work and the work of others, this came as a shock. But after many sleepless nights, further observation and study, and further thought, we redesigned our maps and reconstructed our theory. We started to wonder: Are there times when we do not even need our keys (interventions) to promote solution?

The idea that exceptions might lead us to solution led us to asking the family to describe what happens and what they do when they discover a *dry* bed, and to do so as early in the first session as practically possible. Where before we

had assumed that wet bed and dry beds were alternate ver-
sions of the same pattern, we now start with a simpler assumption: they can be described as *different* patterns. We
assume that both patterns could be described but we are
primarily interested in the dry bed pattern and secondarily
in the differences between the patterns. In fact, once we
know that a dry bed pattern potentially can be described,
because the family mentioned exceptions, we frequently
take the simplest first step: we suggest that they use the
dry bed pattern's behaviors if they should discover a *wet*
bed. In some cases we might make this suggestion even if
we have no idea about the details of any pattern.

CASE EXAMPLE TWO[1]

A family came to therapy in an attempt to help their 10-
year-old son stop wetting bed. Every once in a while, in the
previous six months, they had discovered a dry bed (an exception). However, most nights it was wet. Over the span of
four years they had tried everything but nothing had
worked. Physically there was nothing wrong with the boy
and he had not wet his pants in at least six years (another
exception). Mother, father, and son were unable to describe
any differences between wet bed nights and dry bed nights,
but the six-year-old daughter pointed out that her brother
was dry every Wednesday morning. (A difference had been
noticed.) On Wednesday morning it was father who woke the
boy while mother did it the rest of the week. After dismiss-
ing the children from the session, the therapist suggested
that waking the boy should be father's job during the two-
week interval between sessions. Both parents agreed to this
temporary shift in routine. They also agreed to keep this
plan a secret.

During this entire two-week period the bed was dry. This
was the longest period in the boy's life. However, it was
inconvenient for father to continue waking the boy. The par-

---

[1]The therapy in this case was done without a team.

ents agreed to toss a coin each day for the next two weeks to decide who was going to wake the boy the following morning. Again the bed was dry each morning. During the following month, this plan was modified so that the parents could plan ahead; dad would continue to wake the boy on three or four mornings each week, but they would not let the boy know which ones. It was further agreed that after two dry months, they would reward the boy with the alarm clock he had been asking for. The boy received his alarm on schedule.

What is going on here? How does waking the child influence what has happened the night before? Certainly the boy's knowing that dad would wake him the next morning could have influenced the boy's ability to stay dry. But, on the Friday morning after the first session the boy's bed was dry. The boy did not know dad was going to wake him. If there is a connection between dad's waking the boy on Friday morning and his finding a dry bed, what is it?

The interventions in this case follow a very simple rule: *Once you know what works, do more of it.* The family told the therapist that when dad woke the boy on Wednesday, the bed was dry. This was the only noted exception to the bed-wetting rule (a "rule" like this is only part of the observer's map). The intervention was an attempt to trigger the dry bed pattern. It seems reasonable to expect that the bed would be dry once the boy figured out that it was now dad's job to wake him, but for the bed to be dry on this first day seems inexplicable.

Of course there is no way of knowing what the boy might have imagined that the therapist told his parents and he could only imagine what course of events might occur. Therefore, the surprise of dad's waking him – which the boy associates with a dry bed – might indeed reinforce the dry bed pattern. Perhaps the boy's not knowing what to expect was enough to undermine his own expectation of waking to a wet bed. Once any expectation becomes different, any pattern can change.

For a brief therapist it might be enough to just accept this story as "the way things go" and to remember for future reference that having a different person wake a bed wetter might result in a dry bed.

When asked to explain what was different now that the bed had been dry for awhile, mother said she felt relief at not having to look forward to finding a wet bed the following morning and, therefore, she thought she might be treating the boy differently in the evenings. This dad confirmed, remarking that her different attitude toward the boy had begun immediately after the initial session. There were fewer hassles about the boy's homework and the children's bedtime.

IF IT DOESN'T WORK, DO SOMETHING DIFFERENT

CASE EXAMPLE THREE

A 40-year-old woman, who we will call Mrs. A, was sent to therapy by her dentist because of bruxism. She was unable to recall a single exception: She ground her teeth every night which was giving her headaches, a sore jaw, and abnormal wear on her teeth. Her description of her life sounded essentially "normal" to the therapist. Mrs. A had some gripes about her job, her children, and her husband, but she saw none of these as problematic for her.

The therapist suggested that Mrs. A carry out an experiment. She agreed. He asked her to switch sides of the bed with her husband and to observe closely whatever the results might be. Although puzzled, she confirmed her agreement.

Two weeks later, Mrs. A reported the results. Although neither she nor her husband understood the experiment, they switched sides of the bed. The first night she had some difficulty sleeping but she did not grind her teeth at all. In fact, during the two-week interval she had not ground her teeth once.

Again, what is going on here? What does switching sides of the bed have to do with treating bruxism? What does switching sides of the bed have to do with not grinding teeth? Is this magic rather than therapy? Alchemy rather than science? What is going on when the therapist makes the suggestion, Mrs. A follows it and stops grinding her teeth?

This story is puzzling because people in our culture have long assumed that the nature of the problem determines what the solution needs to be. It is often believed that understanding the problem is the first step in solving it. This assumption seems *logical* and, in fact, it seems more than logical. It seems to lie within the nature of the way things are. Within this framework, it seems that any solution to any problem (i.e., bruxism) needs to have a logical relationship to the nature of the problem. In this case it should be specifically related to the nature of bruxism. But the connection between teeth grinding and sleeping positions seems tenuous at best, absurd and bizarre at worst.

Is this a story about a fluke, a one time event that borders on the miraculous? Or is this an example of an anomaly, something that should lead to a reconsideration of the assumed connections between problems and solutions? If it is not a fluke or a miracle, perhaps it should lead even further, to a reconsideration of what it is that is going on in the therapy situation.

But, what's going on here? The experimental switching sides of the bed is based on some case examples that are part of the oral tradition of brief therapy (cases which are not necessarily part of the published literature). Among brief therapists, stories are told about the experimental switching of sleeping positions being used to solve recurring nightmares, insomnia, snoring, bed wetting, and sexual frequency problems. But the connection between teeth grinding and these other complaints seem only to confuse the issue more if one holds the assumption that solutions need to be logically related to the problem they solve. However, for a brief therapist the connection is obvious: In all these cases the bed and sleeping positions are part of the **context** in which the problems occur.

Another assumption that people in our culture often hold is that one needs to know the cause of a problem in order to solve it. Once you know the cause, you can do something about it which will solve the problem. Therapists in particular often search for causation in unconscious conflicts, past traumas, marital problems, family problems, and/or work problems. While a causal assumption can certainly be useful at times, in the bruxism case (and the other related cases) it is hard to imagine what one's location in bed has to do with causing the problem.

Brief therapists usually do not hold this causal assumption and therefore their work is radically different. Unlike most types of therapy, brief therapy tends to be situation-centered rather than person-centered or even family-centered. That is, whatever the cause of a problem might be, its continuation has something to do with the context or setting in which it occurs and the expectation that the problem is going to continue. A brief therapist might assume that there are subtle cues in the woman's sleeping situation that trigger teeth grinding and therefore could suggest changing that situation.

It is often assumed that problems of whatever sort are maintained by a payoff or reward that the person receives, i.e., continued teeth-grinding assures the continued rewards — whatever they might be. This leads to the idea that Mrs. A needs to develop other ways to generate the same type of rewards in order to stop grinding her teeth.

This assumption may or may not be useful in any particular case. Brief therapists are more likely to assume that problems are simply self-maintaining and that is all there is to it. This assumption leads to the idea that **any** difference in behavior, thoughts, feelings, perceptions, and/or context stands a chance of making a difference such that the complaint is resolved.

Although brief therapists tend not to hold some common assumptions, they are aware that other people do. As far as the brief therapist is concerned, these assumptions are important to a case only if the client holds them. During the therapeutic interview, the therapist will talk with the client about the client's assumptions and his or her intervention will take these into account. For Mrs. A the teeth-grinding was a mystery. She and her dentist could not account for it and nothing they had tried had worked. Given this, an experimental approach seemed reasonable to her.

Since bruxism seems to involve only one person and sexual frequency problems seem to involve two people, they seem more different than similar. In fact, it is often assumed that the number of people involved makes for different kinds of problems and different types of solutions. With this assumption in mind, a couple might seek either a marital therapist or a sex therapist, while the woman reasonably seeks a therapist who is individually focused or a hypnotherapist who might give her some mysterious therapy for her mysterious problem. To further complicate things, parents whose child has nightmares might seek a child therapist or a family therapist (in which case at least three people can be seen as involved in the problem and the solution). Which the parents choose depends on their assumptions about the problem. Based on these assumptions, it would appear obvious that the nightmare problem is different from the teeth grinding problem and both are different from sexual frequency problems.

Yet a brief therapist might suggest some shift in the sleep situation in any or all of the cases. The couple might be asked to swap sides of the bed while the child might be asked to sleep with her head at the foot of the bed or the family might be asked to shift the location of the bed in her room. In all these seemingly disparate examples it is the *context* or the behavioral setting which is seen by the brief therapist as similar in some way and as subject to experimental manipulation and therapeutic intervention. For the brief therapist, behaviors, feelings, thoughts, and perceptions and their specific context are all part of the same pattern, therefore any difference in the context, behavior, thought, feelings, and perception will necessarily have influence on the whole pattern.

Of course, finding solutions is not so simple that switching sleeping positions will work in any specific example of bruxism. The connections between the various elements of any pattern can be seen to take different forms and the various elements are often given different emphasis. What the pattern "means" and what the elements of the pattern "mean" and what the form of the pattern "means" is up to the interpretation of participants and observers. Simply, teeth grinding might mean one thing to Mrs. A, a different thing to her dentist and something else to a brief therapist. Each of the participants constructs a meaning for himself based on what he or she thinks is pertinent to the situation at hand.

At least part of the meaning a situation holds for an individual depends on how other participants construct their meanings for the same situation. The brief therapist's and the dentist's meanings are clearly related to Mrs. A's since they both depend on her for all their information. The dentist will take into consideration his knowledge about teeth, jaws, and muscles while the therapist will take into consideration his knowledge about contexts and human relations.

We might imagine that Mrs. A might be "grinding her teeth" for a battle with her husband, one that she is avoiding. If this were the meaning the situation had for Mrs. A, then the brief therapist would take the marital relationship into account when he thinks about the context of the teeth grinding. The experiment might lead to open conflict between Mr. and Mrs. A, therefore some different task should be given unless Mrs. A is willing to run that risk. The marital relationship is another aspect of the pattern and Mrs. A and the therapist might choose to work on that because Mrs. A is intimately connected to Mr. A and therefore she can influence that relationship almost as easily as she can influence her own sleeping position.

THE SYSTEM UNDER CONSIDERATION

What a therapist does and how he or she thinks about his or her client's situation depends on a map of the situation. From the brief therapist's perspective, Mrs. A's bruxism is somehow connected to:

(a) reports about Mr. A and his advice;
(b) reports about other aspects of the marital relationship;
(c) reports about their children's ideas about the bruxism or about the marriage;
(d) reports about who sleeps where;
(e) reports about the dentist and his advice;
(f) the therapist's experiences;
(g) reports about Mrs. A's ideas about problem solving;
(h) reports about advice from friends;
(i) etc.

All of the participants and the relationships between and among them are all potential building blocks for how the participants construct the meaning of the teeth grinding. This construction informs, limits, or constrains where Mrs. A, her dentist, and her therapist look for solutions. Unfortunately, if Mrs. A were convinced that teeth-grinding is due to one particular aspect of her situation, i.e., a poor marital relationship, then she would only look at that one aspect for potential solutions. As a consequence, this would mean that all other potential solutions—no matter how simple and easy—would be beyond her ken.

4

THEORY CONSTRUCTION: TOWARD A THEORY OF SOLUTION

The purpose of this chapter is to describe the constraints of a theory of brief family therapy, one that is built on viewing therapy-as-a-system. In the field of family therapy the family-as-a-system traditionally has been the system under consideration and the therapy situation-as-a-system[1] has been given far less consideration. The focus of this theory project is on the interactive situation that involves clients, therapist(s), and the context in which they work together.

The relationship between what we do (practice) and how we talk about or describe what we do (theory) continues to be very strong (and recursive) and both of these (theory and practice) are recursively related to our ongoing research. This has been part of our intent for our research and theory construction program since its start in 1978. The current version of a theory of solution is presented in Chapter 6. This chapter and the next (which describe some of the method involved) set the stage for that presentation.

A theory, as I use the term, is not meant as an "explana-

---

[1]This presentation is focused on "brief therapy as a system" but a more general focus on "therapy as a system" is implicit.

tion," rather a theory is only a coherent "description" of specific sequences of events within a specific context. This theory may not be "scientific"[2] enough for some[3] and may be too reductionistic for others.[4] It is, however, rigorous and consistent. I have, of course, continued our tradition (de Shazer, 1982a, 1982b; de Shazer et al., 1985) of keeping the therapist-interacting-with-the-client-in-the-therapy-setting (i.e., the therapy system) in the description or theory of therapy (Tomm, 1986). In fact, a theory of therapy that does not at least implicitly include the therapist would be a theory that is not at all based on direct observation of therapy and would end up at best simply empty or vacuous.

This theory is only meant to describe the various pathways client and therapist together can predictably follow from "complaint" to "goal achievement" and "solution." For instance, when a therapist begins to search for exceptions, then we know that the client has been able to describe a complaint. Furthermore, we can predict that the therapist's *initiating a search for exceptions* will be followed by something we can describe as a successful search or an unsuccessful one. Whether the search is successful or not leads predictably to the next step, etc.

All that a therapist deals with is his construction of how his client constructs his own reality; from these two constructions client and therapist jointly construct a therapeutic reality. The premise behind this, which might be called "radical constructivism" (von Glasersfeld, 1975) or "verbal realism" (Wilder-Mott, 1981), is that to a greater or lesser extent, social reality is constructed through communication.

As Wilder-Mott puts it:

> If one accepts that social reality can be defined quite variously in dialectical interplay with circumstantial constraints, then a rose by any other name be-

[2]What "scientific" might mean in this context depends on how one defines the term and there are various definitions from which to pick.
[3]See, for instance, Shields (1986).
[4]See, for instance, Dell (1985); Keeney (1983); Tomm (1984).

comes something else again. Is a certain behavioral
pattern nagging or reminding? Oppression or loving
protection? (Wilder-Mott, 1981, p. 29).

Communication theorist Barnlund (1981) suggests that

> all meanings, since they are the creation of unique
> persons in unique settings, are distinctive. Further-
> more, that since our knowledge of the world is ines-
> capably subjective, human interaction is about a
> transformed and imaged world. It is not the "real"
> world, but these transforms that we fight about,
> laugh about, cry about. Our meanings are fictions,
> valued and useful fictions, but fictions nonetheless
> (1981, p. 95)

Clearly, communication is an interpersonal process which
implies that these meanings are negotiable. Furthermore,
the context, or the "behavior setting," influences our understanding. For instance, knowing that the situation you are
in is a birthday party for your 14 year old niece and not a
reception for the Pope helps to define expectable and appropriate behavior. The therapy situation *per se* clearly defines
the setting, and any analysis of behavior within that setting
needs to be situation-centered rather than person-centered
or even family-centered.

People behave the way they do in relation to the other
people in the situation and in relation to the context within
which the situation occurs. Both as doers and observers,
meaning is attributed following action. The meaning of a
word or a behavior, for instance, can only be constructed or
invented through how that word is used in social interaction — in a specific context.

DISTINCTION AND DIFFERENCE

The first step in defining the differences between a theory
based on the family-as-a-system and one based on the therapy situation-as-a-system is to *draw a DISTINCTION*. To

spell out my position, I start with refining or redefining a distinction between

(a) the study of the family-as-a-system [a description based on having a separate, objective observer of the family-as-a-system]; and

(b) the study of therapy-as-a-system [a description that includes the therapist/observer as a member of the system under consideration] (de Shazer, 1982a).

What I have to say is said *only* about the ongoing study of therapy-as-a-system that my colleagues and I are involved in, and the descriptions, concepts or theories may or may not apply to Family Therapy. We assume that there is some sort of relationship or fit between "therapy-as-a-system" and Family Therapy, but we do not assume any necessary correspondence. Furthermore, we do not necessarily assume (*a priori*) that the differences between the approaches are the kind of differences that make a difference, and we also do not assume that they do not make a difference.

SCOPE CONDITIONS

Traditionally, theories (of whatever scope) in fields such as family therapy or sociology are constructed out of generalizations or principles or law-schema derived from research findings and/or disciplined observations and/or experimental investigations.

As Berger (Berger, et al., 1977) put it,

a theory-building strategy [of the kind used here] depends upon *scope-defined* models. As explicit definitions of scope conditions are rare, even in formal models, it is useful to comment on their place in theories. The "scope" of a theory consists of assertions describing the features and properties of situations to which the theory is applicable . . . Scope conditions are general theoretical conditions; they limit the application of a theory quite abstractly to a specified number or type of characteristics, of objects of orientation, or of goals. However, they do not make any reference to particulars . . . The assertions defining the scope of a theory are theoretical in the same sense as other assertions of the theory. In point of fact it would be misleading to imply that somehow the substance of a model was one thing, its scope something else. Scope assertions are as much a part of "the theory proper" as are its basic assumptions about the phenomena within its scope (p. 27).

At this point my focus is the continuing study of therapy-as-a-system, with a particular emphasis on a theory of solution which is seen to apply under the following scope conditions:

(1) The people who are interacting:
    (a) have a task orientation (a complaint is described and recognizable goals are established or, at least, can be established and/or criteria are established for disbanding the system); and
    (b) have a collective orientation (all the participants are involved in the effort to reach the goal(s)).
(2) The physical location or setting includes a therapy room that is connected to an observation room by
    (a) a one-way screen;
    (b) an inter-com;
    (c) video taping and/or audio taping equipment; and
    (d) a door.
(3) The therapy is done by a team including
    (a) one therapist who is in the room with the client;
    (b) and one or more other therapists who are behind the mirror, sometimes including
    (c) supervisors, consultants, and
    (d) researchers.
(4) The client is
    (a) an individual; or
    (b) a couple; or
    (c) a family unit; or

(d) a member or members of a family unit; or

(e) a member or members of a work unit; etc.,

who have made a request for help in resolving some complaint.

These scope conditions apply only to our study of therapy-as-a-system. The theory we are constructing does not necessarily apply to doing therapy in the natural setting, i.e., in an office without a mirror, team, etc. – even when the therapist is deliberately applying what we have learned during our studies. We assume that there is a relationship between the theory construction situation and the natural setting, but this cannot be known for sure since any observation would change the natural setting. However, if it does not apply, then our study should be scrapped without further ado. Many of the cases described in this book were done without a team and represent the application of the theory in clinical practice.

(Although the family therapy focus is different, it is readily apparent that the scope conditions could usefully be applied by an observer to many family therapy institutes. However, the "client" and the relationships between the various elements might need to be defined differently.)

THEORIZING

Any theoretical thinking about therapy-as-a-system needs to fit within these scope conditions. That is, the scope conditions define the constraints of the "system under consideration." Each of the elements and the relationships between and among elements needs to be taken into consideration. Any other elements involved in theoretical thinking are either extraneous and should be eliminated or they need to be added to the scope conditions. (For instance, the regular use of co-therapists [two therapists at the same time] in the room with the client is outside the scope of our theory. If co-therapists were to be involved, then we would have the choice of redefining the theory [i.e., there are always two therapists in the room or, under certain specified conditions, there are always two therapists in the room] or of excluding that event from our study. If it were a common practice then it should be included, but if it were a rare event then it could be excluded [at least for the time being, although it should become the subject of further study]. Rare events are not discarded but are saved for future reference because, if the events become more common, the theory will at least need to be revised or perhaps even discarded.) Should an expert system eventually be placed "on line," i.e., should it actually be used in deciding on what to do, then it would need to be added to the scope conditions.

A quick glance at "scope conditions" reveals that people (with various roles), machines, physical objects, and a collective task are all included: The context, setting and the behaviors within that setting are all related parts of the "system under consideration." It is not just the people and the relationships between and among them that comprise the "system under consideration." The setting itself is part of the "system" and part of what we need to consider when describing what it is that is going on.

Obviously, some sort of "system theory" would seem useful to this project. However, the most typical form of system theory in the therapy world is known as "family systems theory," which is about how families can be described as "systems." This version places a boundary around "the family" as the system under consideration.

Since the system under consideration here is broader, i.e., not limited to "family members and the relations between and among them," a more general version of system theory will prove more useful. Therefore, we draw a distinction between family systems theory—the study of the family-as-a-system—and cybernetics—the study of systemic pattern and form.

Of course, there is nothing to say that our theory is the only one that will fit within the scope conditions. It is merely one theory among many potential theories that might be equally viable—within the same constraints. As we see it, our theory remains viable as long as our experiences fit within the constraints and, pragmatically, as long as it achieves our purposes. This does not make it any "better" than any other theory that might fit within the scope conditions, it just means that our theory has not failed to survive our experiences during the study of therapy-as-a-system.

Von Glasersfeld (1981) put it this way:

> Empiricists and statisticians have long been telling us that we can never "prove" a theory — we can only disprove it. In my terms that means that while we can know when a theory or model knocks against the constraints of our experiential world, the fact that it does *not* knock against them but "gets by" and is still viable, does in no way justify the belief that the theory or model therefore depicts a "real world" (p. 93).

By drawing this distinction between a theory of therapy based on the family-as-a-system and one based on cybernetics, I am not suggesting a dualist view — *either* family therapy *or* brief therapy, nor am I urging a split along the lines of *either* "general systems theory" *or* "cybernetics" — however much such distinctions might appeal to a sense of order. Simply, the distinctions allow us to see both similarities and differences.

OUTSIDE THE SCOPE CONDITIONS

It is important to remember that a scope defined theory says nothing whatsoever about things that are not within the scope conditions. The scope conditions define what is within the domain of inquiry and everything else is considered outside this domain. Clearly a lot of topics, issues and concerns of many people in the fields involved in doing therapy (of any sort) are beyond the scope of this theory. This is fully intentional: the theory is only about therapy-as-a-system.

This restriction may seem severe and perhaps extreme

but it does allow the theorist, researcher, and therapist to have a well defined situation in which to study therapy. Although interaction is part of what we study, the theory construction situation is not as well controlled as a human interaction research laboratory. What goes on during a session is almost free-form and natural and, therefore, the constraints are necessary so that unobserved things do not overly "contaminate" our descriptions. Again, this brings up the question: *"What is it that is going on here?"* Isn't therapy supposed to help clients solve the problems that they are having in their day-to-day living? Well, only sort of.

Traditionally, therapists have thought they had to penetrate the clinical situation, to see beneath or beyond the appearances. This is based on the assumption that the *essence* is hidden away (in the psyche or in the system?). However, other assumptions are possible. Perhaps nothing is hidden away and everything lies in plain view (like Poe's purloined letter) and what is needed and useful is a clear view of what it is that is going on. Something seems hidden because of the familiarity and simplicity of what is in plain view and the conundrum brought about by attempting to look beneath when there is no beneath there.

Miller (1986) suggests that "troubles, solutions, fit and change" can all be "viewed as humanly produced and, therefore, as artifacts of therapeutic practice" (p. 11) and that clients' troubles can best be viewed as constructions dealing with aspects of their social lives which are produced by them in concrete social relationships and settings. From this sociology of trouble perspective, whatever is going on in the therapy situation is simply something that the various participants construct.

This idea is related to the notion that the observer influences what he observes, but goes radically far beyond that. In the therapy situation, the therapist not only observes what the clients say and do and thus influences that; he or she also helps the clients create what they talk about and what they do by asking questions and making comments. In a very real sense, therapists and clients cooperate in constructing the therapeutic reality in which they work together. Simply, the therapy system involves the therapist and client in reconstructing these aspects in such a way that the clients no longer find them troublesome.

5

BUILDING A THEORY: NOTES ON METHOD

Our theory construction process[1] began with a technique known as "thick description." This procedure involves the observers in describing the (observed) therapy sessions or videotapes (or any sequences of events) in as many different ways as possible, from as many different points of view as possible. Looking at the resulting abundance of descriptors, the theorists and researchers then searched for consistencies in the descriptions of the patterns from the various sessions so that a "map" or "family tree" of solution focused interviews could be developed.[2] Once these "family resemblances" (Wittgenstein, 1968) were identified, the researchers began to look for the various branches of the family tree.

FAMILY RESEMBLANCE

Since not all interviews are identical, we found[3] Wittgenstein's "family resemblances concept" to be useful. Except

[1]This was prior to our development of BRIEFER I. In fact, the work with the expert system developed from this process and is dependent upon it.
[2]We have also found this technique useful in teaching therapists interviewing skills while still teaching them about research and theory construction. For example, three videotapes of first sessions (one each by Brian Cade, John H. Weakland, and Steve de Shazer) are thickly described and these descriptions are searched for similarities and differences that might make a difference.
[3]"Solution Focused Interviews" is not necessarily a family resemblance

for identical twins, most family members only share some characteristics. People say that a new baby, for instance, has the father's nose, mother's hair, Uncle Charlie's chin, etc. They seem to mean that these are marks or signs of family membership. The baby's sister may have father's nose, Uncle Charlie's chin, and Aunt Mattie's eyes. Observers might, however, fail to point out that both children have ears like those of the man next door.

It is not a matter of patterns being somehow "the same" or even that the descriptions of the patterns the interviews follow being "the same," but rather the descriptions include "a complicated network of similarities overlapping and criss-crossing: sometimes overall similarities, sometimes similarities of details" (Wittgenstein, 1968, 66)[4] which identifies the family tree based on resemblances. The common descriptors are not some sort of "universals" or "essenses," but more like the similarities between a musical theme and its variations. A multiplicity of examples is perhaps the only way to explain what is meant by the concept of *solution-focused interviews*. This is analogous to indicating a place by pointing rather than drawing boundaries.

Wittgenstein uses the concept of "game" to illustrate "family resemblance concepts." Although we know somehow what a game is, a unified definition is impossible. Therefore, one must string together a series of examples. If one describes first baseball, then chess, certain descriptors will be added while others will drop out (i.e., chess pieces and balls). Then, if one adds solitaire other descriptors will be added while some are dropped, i.e., here the competition between players. Then, does one add practicing basketball by oneself in the driveway? We can certainly recognize this as game-like even though there is no winning and no losing (Wittgenstein 1968, 67-71): It certainly bears a family resem-

---

concept as Wittgenstein defined the term. Certainly there is a similarity: there is no simple unitary definition and the best explanation is by a series of examples.
[4]References to Wittgenstein's *Philosophical Investigations* are by paragraph number rather than page number.

blance to basketball and therefore to other games. Like
other family resemblances concepts, there is no clear-cut
boundary around "games."

Another illustration: Geometric figures, drawn with
straight lines, belong to the same family tree. For instance,
a rectangle and a triangle have some family resemblances.

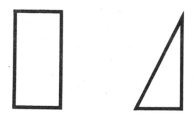

They readily fit together and, importantly, a diamond shape
would fit with either or both.

In fact, the concept of "fit" is a good example of a family
resemblance concept. Although the triangle and the rectangle have two sides which can be described as isomorphic and
therefore fit together, the diamond – which is not isomorphic
with either – fits with either or both equally as well as the
triangle and the rectangle fit together.

PATTERN

Pattern description is one way of establishing family resemblance, but pattern recognition is not necessarily easy.
At times the two patterns (of descriptions) do not have a

high degree of one-to-one correspondence. The level of similarity can be rather abstract.

The following example, borrowed from Douglas Hofstadter (1981), illustrates the process of pattern recognition quite clearly.

Sequence A: 1234554321
Sequence B: 12344321

Do these two sequences follow the same pattern? What is to B as 4 is to A?
The usual answer is the "3" on each side of the pair of 4s.

Sequence C: 11223344544332211

Does C follow the same pattern? If so, what is to C as 4 is to A? Intuitively, it seems to somehow follow the same pattern, or some sort of variation on the pattern. The most typical answer is the "44" on each side of the single 5. Thus the sequence has been punctuated this way: 11–22–33–44–5–44–33–22–11. Interestingly, the sequence can be punctuated differently: 11–22–33–44544–33–22–11, and the answer becomes the "33" on each side of the 44544 as the "central group"! The question in all three sequences is: What serves as the pivot point?

Interview patterns sometimes do not behave this well, and the researchers can get stuck trying to figure out an apparently different type of pattern:

Sequence D: 12345678
Sequence E: 1357654321

These sequences might identify specific branches of the same family since they share the "1234" or "4321" motion, or they might identify different "family trees" or an anomaly since D does not pivot and return to the starting point. Only other non-pivoting sequences that form similar patterns and the presence of other similarities will allow the researcher or theoretician to make that decision. This is analogous to the question (above) about whether or not practicing basketball alone in the driveway belongs to the family of games.

As we have seen, one branch of the family tree can be recognized by describing the therapist as working with the client to "define the differences between the complaint and the exceptions." Clearly this does not happen in all sessions since not every session includes a description of a successful "search for useful exceptions." The researchers then look at their wealth of descriptions and search for any differences that further identify this as a distinct branch of the family tree. In this way, the researchers attempt to have their map include any differences that seem to make a difference.

For instance, when the "differences between the exceptions and the complaint" are described, this is frequently followed by the therapist's giving the client a task that incorporates these differences. However, when the "differences" are not described, the therapist frequently gives the client a task that asks the client to predict daily whether the next day would follow the exception pattern or the complaint pattern. Since neither of these tasks are used when the "search for useful exceptions" failed, branches of the family tree can be clearly identified and described.

CHANGE TALK

In a broad sense, the rationale for therapy is "change" — the client comes to therapy wanting to solve his problem. Within this framework, clients depict their problem, a process that is shaped interactively by the conversation between them and the therapist. It is this depiction or construction that therapy deals with, and therefore a primary focus of the interview is on helping clients change their way of constructing their (problematic) experience. Thus, if the interview starts with the client talking about being depressed all the time and ends with the client talking about being depressed only 80% of the time, then that particular interview has been successful.

In some senses, the interview can be simply described in this way:

The client is like a writer who is very unhappy with the ending of the chapter on which he is currently working. He tells his concerns to his editor who looks at what has been written so far and then, because the editor comes to it fresh, he is able to suggest alternate endings. It is then up to the author to decide which if any of the suggestions are viable or fit for him. Frequently, just hearing that there are alternate endings is enough to help the author overcome his unhappiness with the work. Of course the editor then has become a sort of co-author because the ending is based on his having provided alternate views of the author's reality.

Clients are constructing their lives and it is the therapist's task to help them "get on with life" in a way that they will find satisfactory. Of course, there are many possible and useful constructions that will fit for any client in any situation. The specific construction is, perhaps, unimportant. What matters is that the client finds the solution she and the therapist build to be a satisfactory one. This view assumes that a change in the way clients construct their experience, as reflected in how they report it or talk about it, will promote their having a different experiences which, in turn, will prompt different depictions or reports in subsequent sessions.

This suggests that the interview is a construction or depiction of the client's "problem," the purpose of which is to bring about change in the situation the client depicts. Since the interview is really just a conversation, the change referred to is more accurately thought of as "talk of change" or simply "change talk" (Gingerich et al., 1987). Change talk may consist of client reports of how things have changed outside the therapy setting, or change talk may consist of observable changes in how the client depicts the situation within the therapy setting. In either case, talk about change is the purpose of the interview (Gingerich et al., 1987) and the purpose of homework tasks is to help the client construct his experience differently and thus transform his depictions of his situation, i.e., increased change talk in subsequent sessions.

Frequently clients state their complaints in this way:

"I am depressed."
"I am anxious."
"I am bulimic."

This "I am x" statement is similar in form to:

"I am redheaded."
"I am male."
"I am French."

The latter statements using the "I am x" form describe a "steady state" attribute and the similarities to the former, caused by using the same form, can fool us into thinking that they are "the same thing." That is, the "I am" signals parallel descriptions and, therefore, "depression," "anxiety," and "bulimia" can become mistakenly seen as immutable states like "redheaded," "male," and "French." As Wittgenstein (1958) put it, "When words in our ordinary language have prima facie analogous grammars we are inclined to try to interpret them analogously; i.e., we try to make the analogy hold throughout" (p. 7).

Curiously, when asked to explain how they know that they are depressed, clients will frequently mention occasional "up days." Thus being depressed is defined, in part, by not being depressed. Within the client's logic, exceptions should not occur because that would be like a person defining being French by being not French.

However, these "up days" are not seen as a difference that makes a difference. The "up days" are dismissed as trivial when the problem is framed as "being depressed." It seems that they are misled by the form of their statement, "I am depressed" and its similarity to the statement "I am French." However, once the exceptions, the "up days," are reconstructed into differences that do make a difference, then they can lead to a satisfactory solution. Once there is doubt, once the exception is seen to make a difference, the client can change the form or grammar of his statement to "At times I feel depressed." This change talk then allows or permits the client to also, at times, not feel depressed.

Process Research

The development of the concept of change talk led to some research on therapist-client interaction during the interview (Gingerich et al., 1987). If change talk was what the therapist was trying to develop during the session, then we wanted to know what client and therapist alike did that was useful in promoting change talk. A coding scheme related to Gottman's (1979) was developed which included therapist codes and client codes.

THERAPIST CONTENT CODES

I   Information gathering/session maintenance
  –Ask client to describe/explain problem
  –Include maintenance tasks, i.e., summarizing, clarification, socializing, etc.
  –Include changes the client describes which the therapist does not appear to recognize as change
  –When asking specifically about positive change, code as E
C   Change-inducing interventions
  –Reframes, i.e., therapist suggests a different way of viewing the clients' situation . . . therapist asserts this is a difference that makes a difference . . . includes normalizing, identifying and labeling change, establishing a "yes set," etc.
  –Behavior change, i.e., therapist asks what client will do differently (in the future) when goal is achieved or says "do something different"
  –Code C when therapist is attempting to induce change IN THE FUTURE
E   Elicit report of change/homework/exceptions

--Ask client to report, clarify or elaborate on positive change
--Ask client for exception to the problem
--Ask client to explain "world view"
--E refers to change that has ALREADY OCCURRED

A   Amplify or reinforce positive change ("cheerleading")
--Code A when therapist amplifies or reinforces change client has reported or demonstrated
--Therapist praises or compliments change the CLIENT HAS RE-PORTED AND ACKNOWLEDGED
--A is often in the form of an exclamation

G   Negotiate goals/signs of positive change
--Code G when the therapist is trying to get the client to specify or agree to a goal
--Negotiates how much change is necessary
--Includes renegotiating goals in later sessions

CLIENT CONTENT CODES

I   Information/maintainance/business
--Problem continues/no positive change
--Small talk
--Explaining or asking therapist to explain problem

C   Positive change in the problem and/or in other areas
--Client describes/reports positive change in th problem/situation
--Client explains/clarifies positive change
--Client describes/reports positive change in how he/she views the problem
--Client describes/reports *recognized* exceptions to the problem pattern
--Code C when client describes how things used to be in order to explain how things are now different
--When client describes how things could be different but conveys *no expectation* that they will be different, code I

U   Unrecognized positive change
--Client reports change but does not appear to recognize it as such
--Reports unrecognized exceptions to the problem

G   Client specifies goal/signs of change
--Client describes how things will be different, i.e., negotiates goals/signs of change

–Code G only if client indicates belief in or intention to achieve goals

Y "Yes set"

–Client shows acceptance of the message the therapist is about to deliver

–Client shows an open frame of mind to what the therapist is saying

Interviews were then coded from transcripts and watching the videotape of the sessions; interrater reliability was established and then the patterns of codes were studied.

RESEARCH CHANGES PRACTICE

Analysis of sessions conducted prior to this project revealed that client change talk (C) was common in the second and subsequent sessions but rare in the first. Client information (I) was predominate in the first session. It was noted that change talk was over four times more likely to occur after the therapist attempted to elicit (E) change talk and was more likely to continue after the therapist responded in a positive way (A).

Analysis of sessions conducted during this project revealed that client change talk (C), therapist elicit (E) and amplify (A) were happening much more frequently in the first session than they were before. As a result, client information (I) was occurring less than before.

A rigorous search for exceptions and for how the client will know that the problem is solved have both been found useful in promoting client change talk in the first session. As a result, we have dispensed with much of what we had been doing in initial sessions and began to elicit change talk instead. This eliminates most of the usual first session. Second session behaviors of both client and therapist moved into the first session. Before this project, the average number of sessions per client was six; after, it is five (de Shazer et al., 1986). We cannot be sure that this decrease is due to this project.

What Is Not on the Map

Like any map, it is important to remember that the map is not the territory. Our map (or family tree of solution-focused interviews) is similar to a highway map that tells us little or nothing about detours, elevation, types of terrain, hills and valleys, and unpaved roads (which may, however, turn out to be both useful and interesting). To switch metaphors, maps of this type are like towns: One can never say that a town is complete or incomplete. That is, the map excludes the descriptors that did not seem to make a difference and/or what seemed to be idiosyncratic to a particular therapy session. (These rare or unique events have been noted as "potential anomalies" that may prompt us to revise the map and introduce a further branching.) Thus, on this map, there is nothing about the interviewing techniques that the therapists use to help clients "search for exceptions to the rules of the complaint." Similarly, there is nothing about how therapists and clients went about "describing the differences between exceptions and complaints," and there is nothing to indicate whether or not client and therapist talked about the past or the physiological aspects of the complaint vs the sociological aspects.

The map is "*de*-scriptive" rather "*pre*-scriptive." It describes what solution focused therapists *do* rather than what they should do. Thus, it is not a map of the "right way," or the "only way," or even the "best way." It is simply a map of the way therapists at BFTC behave during an interview that indicates there is a family resemblance between various "solution focused" interviews. Importantly, this map also does not tell us anything about what might be a "wrong way" to construct a solution focused interview, i.e., just because it is not mentioned does not mean it might not be useful for the client and therapist to do it.

The *central map* (see the following chapter) and the various sectional maps or diagrams based on that map are the result of using the thick description technique with many cases and of process research. Obviously, enough interviews need to be watched so that the observers are overwhelmed with the sameness before they are able to see any differences or to receive news of difference. Because of this, we can have some confidence that what is the *same* about our descriptions from interview to interview is really descriptive and not hypothetical or based on premature generalizations built on "the way things should be."[5]

[5]See also Chapter 2 in regard to this confidence.

6

A THEORY OF SOLUTION

Although we call our family tree of solution-focused interviews a "map"—because it looks like one—it is more properly
called a theory.[1] This theory of solution was built within our
scope conditions using the methods described in the previous chapters. It is based on our descriptions of similarities
and difference in our descriptions of therapeutic interviews
at BFTC. The theory includes a simple set of propositions
used as principles of description for a solution focused model
of brief therapy. The theory, or map, is an attempt to describe what we do rather than prescribe what should be
done, although the map (a representation of the theory of
solution) can be used as a decision tree providing that the
user remembers that the map is not the territory. Much of
what happens in any specific session might not be included
on the map, i.e., there is no description of the procedures
that might be useful in the search for exceptions. This type
of description is found in other chapters where the sections
of the map are looked at in detail.

Theories and maps are a lot alike in many important re-
spects. Like a map, the aim of a theory is not to assert

---

[1]The term "theory" is often used rather loosely by family therapists. Theoretical thinking, such as Dell (1985), Keeney (1983), and Tomm (1984),
might best be called metatheory or epistemology rather than theory. This
work, although valuable in thinking about therapy, lacks the specificity
needed for it to be called theory.

something about the domain but rather to present it in a perspicuous way. The assertions come in the explications or descriptions of the map, i.e., theoretical thinking. Like a map, a theory will contain elements that are *not* empirical or pragmatic. But these are not assertions at all, but rather they belong to the apparatus used to represent the domain. All the "facts," "data," "structures," and "laws" which are elements of a theory are assembled descriptions, or formulations, or constructions – interpretations. There are no "facts," or "data," or "structures," or "laws" as such; there are only assemblages. Strictly speaking, there is always only construction or interpretation.

READING THE MAP

At the top of the map are coded descriptions of three types of relationships which are usefully distinguished from each other. Unfortunately, the codes appear to label the clients instead of the interaction between therapist and client. But that is the way maps are: a big blob is often used to represent San Francisco and, as we all know, there is nothing blobbish about that city. The code names for these relationships are just ways used to represent part of the domain the theory covers. As any therapy session develops, particularly as the first session develops, therapist and client construct a relationship based on the task at hand. Misunderstanding that relationship or describing it in the wrong way can easily lead to trouble of one kind or another. For instance, telling a mother to deliver her child to school even though the child is crying will probably not be a useful intervention if the mother believes that it is the child who needs to get herself to school and that she, the mother, does not need to do anything to make that happen.

THERAPIST-CLIENT RELATIONSHIP PATTERNS

As a result of the interview various types of therapist-client relationships develop that can be usefully described as fitting into one of three groups. The general term "client" is

THE CENTRAL MAP

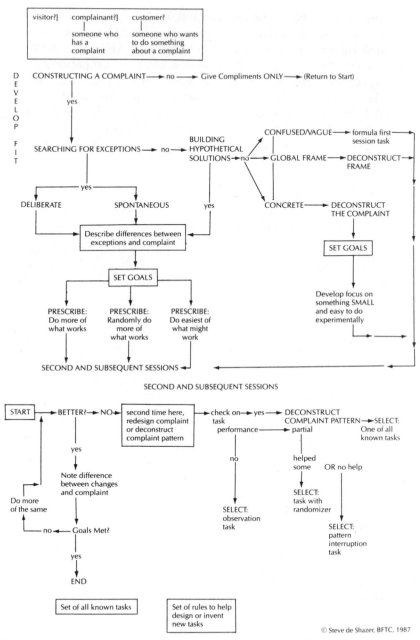

© Steve de Shazer, BFTC, 1987

applied to "visitors," "complainants," and "customers" alike. It would be a misreading to equate this distinction with ascriptions of "motivation" or "readiness for therapy" or to any traits of the client. "Visitors" must have somebody to visit with, "complainants" somebody to complain to, and "customers" somebody from which to buy. The "labels" are solely meant to give the observer a thumbnail description of the relationship between the therapist and her client.

Visitors?

Sometimes people seem to have no complaints and their reason for being in the therapist's office is simply that someone told them to come or someone brought them. In this situation the person with the complaint might not be in the therapist's office at all. It may be a probation or parole officer, a judge, a school principal, a spouse or a parent who has sent the person to see a therapist. The coercion may be explicit, i.e., a court order, or it may be implicit, i.e., an unspoken threat of divorce.

Since there is no complaint to work on, therapy cannot begin (this situation is outside the theory's scope conditions) and therefore it is a mistake for the therapist to try to intervene no matter how obvious the "problem" may be to an observer. With "visitors" like this, any intervention is likely to be rejected and, thus, the therapist's error in not recognizing these people as visitors sets up a classic "resistant relationship" between him and the other people in the office.

At one time or another, every therapist is faced with this type of situation and needs to do something useful instead up setting up a problematic relationship. Simply thinking about the situation as "visiting" may be more useful than the therapist's thinking she has "involuntary clients" whom she has to convince that they really need therapy. (Of course if there is an "involuntary client," there is also an "involuntary therapist" which makes the whole situation difficult.) Cooperation is unlikely when the visitors are saying that they do not need therapy but the therapist is thinking and saying that they do.

Fortunately, our way of interviewing can be useful in this situation and several of our guidelines suggest what to do.

(1) Be as nice as possible.
(2) The therapist in the room is *always* on the side of the people being interviewed.
(3) Look for what works rather than what does not.

If, for instance, a family is in the office because the juvenile probation officer sent them, they often appear to resent this order. This is particularly salient when the parents think that the whole problem is the child's, not theirs. Sometimes this can be a starting point for developing a complaint. "The p.o. is on our back; how do we get him off our backs?" Therapy then can be done around their proving to the p.o. that they do not need to come to therapy. How can they prove this to him? Only by changing – and thus therapy can begin. However, this sort of contract is usually not developed in the first session. Therefore, we have found it useful to give visitors a series of compliments but no task at the end of the first session. Not infrequently, somebody will remark that "this is the first time a professional ever said anything nice to me." And thus *fit* is starting to develop and a viable complaint might be brought up in the following session.

Complainants?

A therapeutic conversation can be punctuated as beginning with a complaint. No matter how fuzzy, vague, global, or specific, any complaint is a sign that the therapist and the other participants can begin therapy. Thus "complainant" is a code name for a business-like relationship, one in which the client has developed some expectation of solution as a result of the interview. In general terms, the task at hand is clear to everybody involved. Of course, if the therapist is conversing with a couple or a family, some of the relationships may be given the code name "visitor" while others are given the code name "complainant." When this is the case, the therapist can only expect that the people who are relating to her as complainants are part of therapy. The visitor/complainant distinction suggests, therefore, that the complainants can be given tasks with which they will cooperate. When a visitor performs a task, that is an unanticipated bonus and the therapist needs to revise her view toward that relationship. Sometimes continuing to invite the visitor(s) to sessions impedes therapy or confuses things for everybody and therefore it might be useful to only invite the complainant(s) to the following session.

Customers?

When during the course of a session the complainant clearly indicates that he or she is not only willing but wants to *do something* about the complaint, then the therapist-client relationship is given the code name "customer." Primarily, customers are distinguished from other complainants solely because of the way the customer describes his situation and his goals. In these situations, the therapist can give behavioral tasks with a high degree of confidence that the customer will do the task and find it useful. Again, when the therapist is conversing with a couple or a family, some of the people may be "complainants" while others are "customers" and each type of relationship indicates what kind of task will fit: for customers, behavioral tasks and for complainants, observational or thinking tasks.

Of course during a series of sessions these relationships change and develop. Visitors can become complainants, and complainants can become customers, while customers can become complainants. How they describe previous task performance is a good clue. If the response is reported in behavioral terms, then behavioral tasks might prove useful. If the response is reported in perceptual or conceptual terms, then non-behavioral tasks are probably more likely to fit.

DEVELOPING FIT

Along the left side of the map is another blob-like entry labeled "developing fit." This just represents another aspect of the domain without in any way explaining what is meant. Although what to do in the interview that leads to an appropriate intervention can be drawn as a decision tree, that is not all there is to it. Somehow the therapist must decide how to deal with the people he or she is having a conversation with. With visitors, complainants, and customers alike, the therapist is responsible for what happens during the session. It is not a casual conversation as might be had with these people in a local pub.

Throughout the session, the therapist needs to be developing a fit with the person or people she is interviewing. This kind of relationship, although temporary for the duration of therapy, involves a special kind of closeness, responsiveness, or harmony. When fit is established, all the participants pay close attention to what the others are saying. In its most extreme form, the hypnotic subject is only responsive to the voice of the hypnotist (called "being in rapport"). Fit is a mutual process involving both therapist and the people he is conversing with during which they come to trust each other, pay close attention to each other, and accept each other's worldview as valid, valuable, and meaningful. By accepting the client's worldview the therapist is able to be useful and help resolve the complaint as simply and easily as possible:

There once was this hospital patient who said he was Jesus Christ. After talking with him awhile about the various gifts God gave this world, it so happened that the lab needed book cases and so, Milton Erickson remarked to this patient that of course [since he was Jesus] he had experience as a carpenter. He then built some bookcases and became the lab's handyman. (Haley, 1973)

It is a lot easier to describe fit than it is to tell someone how to develop it. It certainly includes the therapist behaving in such a way that it is clear to his client that he (the client) has everything needed to solve the problem. The only difficulty is that clients do not know that they know how to solve their problems. As Erickson said many times to clients, "Your conscious mind is very intelligent and your unconscious mind is a hell of a lot smarter than you are."

A young, single mother came to therapy complaining about her eight-year-old daughter's sudden outbursts of temper. As the conversation flowed over two sessions, they came up with the idea that mother could get a squirt gun and, when next the daughter had a tantrum, mother would squirt her between the eyes. Both mother and therapist laughed about the image of the shocked little girl.

In the following session, mother reported buying a squirt gun and filling it. She was really ready to squirt her daughter because the tantrums "pissed her off." For several days, mother carried the squirt gun, ready to use. But, when the daughter threw a tantrum, all mother was able to do was laugh at her mental image of the squirted daughter. The tantrum was quickly over, perhaps because the little girl was curious about her laughing mother.

When mother told this story to her therapist, he laughed at the image of mother laughing at the image of her soaking wet daughter.

In spite of the fact that mother never actually squirted her daughter, the task was a success. The therapist accepted that, for whatever reason or reasons, mother knew how best to use that task in her situation. She had trusted her therapist enough to buy and load the squirt gun, but then she trusted herself on how best to use it. When there is a fit, the therapist can trust that the client will use the task to her best advantage.

Mrs. Y was having difficulty making phone calls that were necessary for the performance of her job. She liked everything else about her job and was, in general, quite successful at it. But making these phone calls would potentially make her quite a bit more successful.

After Mrs. Y described how she would like things to be once the problem was solved, the therapist simply told her that "what you've tried has not worked and so, tomorrow, when you get to work, do something different." Mrs. Y smiled and asked "Is that all?" "That's it," I said.

Two weeks later Mrs. Y reported that every day she went to work one hour earlier than was usual or necessary for her. This had not been a conscious decision, but had come about spontaneously. However, since nobody else was there to gossip with, she had nothing to do *except make the phone calls*. Which she did.

What Mrs. Y did differently was something she, on some level, decided to do. Obviously, it was the right thing to do since it worked for her by putting herself in a position to do what she wanted and needed to do.

The search for exceptions allows the therapist to focus the conversation on what the client is doing that is right or useful and therefore fit can usually be developed with relative ease. Obviously, it is much more pleasant for everyone involved to talk about the positive side of things. By assuming that the client is going to form a cooperative relationship, by searching for exceptions, and by always being on the client's side, fit can develop rapidly in the first session.

SET GOALS

Fit is promoted when goals are established to help determine how the client and therapist alike will know when the problem is solved. Without this step, therapy could reasonably go on forever. It might be more useful, in fact, to think about setting up ways to measure goal achievement rather than to just set goals because, with some frequency, the client is able to find a way to determine that therapy has been successful and he or she is more satisfied when something new or different happens that was not thought of as a possible measure of success. Therefore, although brief therapy is goal-directed, the goal is best thought of as some member of the class of ways that the therapist and client will know that the problem is solved rather than any particular member of that class.

Setting specific goals clearly influences outcome (Locke, Shaw, Saari, and Latham, 1981) and, in particular, goals that the client perceives as attainable and difficult are more apt to be met (Bandura and Schunk, 1981; Deci, 1975; Latham and Baldes, 1975; Locke et al., 1981) than vague or easy to meet goals. Particularly when the complaint is vague and/or when no exceptions have been described, establishing goals promotes opening the door to solution.

CASE EXAMPLE FOUR[1]

A young lady came to therapy because she was "insanely jealous." She wanted to cease being jealous and her boyfriend of three years also wanted her to stop being jealous. As she saw it, her jealousy was threatening to break them up but she wanted to marry him. She was unable to describe any times when she did not feel jealous of his friends (male and female), his time away from her, and his interests outside of being with her.

[1]The therapy in this case was done without a team.

Her first response to the miracle question continued to be based on her internal states without reference to any outside manifestations. It was only when the therapist asked her "How will he (her boyfriend) know when the jealousy problem is solved?" that any behavioral descriptions were elicited.

(1) If even a day were to go by when she did not call him. (She sometimes called him 14 times in a day.) She was convinced that if he were to call her more often, she would feel better about the relationship and therefore be less jealous.
(2) If she were to smile and converse with his friends in a social setting instead of pouting.
(3) If she were to go out with her friends instead of staying home alone when she did not go out with him.
(4) Her friends would know if she did not talk only about him when she talked to them.

The following diagram is the section of the central map used to describe this case example. Sections of the central map not used in this case have been eliminated for the sake of clarity.

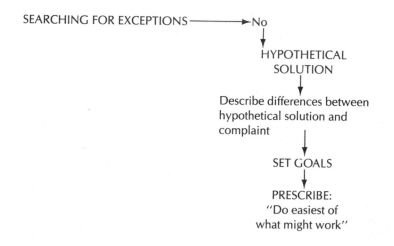

In this case, the theory can be interpreted in this way based on questions derived from BRIEFER II.

(1) Is there a complaint?
Yes
(2) Is there an exception?
No
(3) Is there a hypothetical solution?
Yes
Then, describe differences between the complaint and the hypothetical solution—which also sets the goal. Under these conditions the theory suggests that the therapist prescribe, as a task, the "easiest" or the best described part of the hypothetical solution.

(The section maps throughout the remainder of the book show how the therapist and/or team disciplined their observations about the particular therapy sessions being described and are meant to help illustrate the application of the theory to the particular case examples.)

Any or all of these four signs are adequate goals, i.e., ways to know the problem is solved, and adequate objectives for a task. Simply, it could be suggested that she:

(1) Not call him, or
(2) Smile at his friends, or
(3) Go out with her friends, or
(4) When with her friends, not talk about him to them.

Possibility 1 does not call for any cooperation from other people and, therefore, might have top priority. Options 2, 3, and 4 all call for minimal cooperation from other people and therefore are not first choice for the therapist to assign as a task. Number 2 calls for going out with him and being in a context where there are friends of his which gives her less control over her performing the task, while #3 and #4 depend on her being with her friends. Option 1, if successful, also gives her a chance at getting something she wants – his calling her more often.

She was asked to pick "the easiest one for her" from the

list and she reported, in the second session, that she had decided not to call him. She had a nervous four days during which she had begun to think that perhaps he really did not care, but on the fifth day he called and they went out. She felt better about the relationship and thought that he did too. Since the date on the fifth day she had not called him even once, but he had called her.

It was again recommended that she do the "easiest" one and when he next called she said "no" to his offer to take her out, saying she had plans to go out with her friends that evening. Subsequently, he called every day and had once sent her flowers.

Since she had described so well four signs that would allow him to know that the jealousy problem was solved and since any of the four were quite workable, letting her pick the easiest gave her a greater sense of control which seemed important since she saw the jealousy as "out of control."

Tasks can be readily designed when the client's description of a *hypothetical solution* includes enough behavioral details (i.e., concrete and specific goals) that can be given as tasks much as if they were exceptions. When this use of the crystal ball technique (Erickson, 1954; de Shazer, 1978a, 1985) includes more than one example and they are all tenable, then the therapist can suggest that the client do the one that is the easiest. In this example, none of the four choices are excluded because the new behavior entirely depends on other people's initiation or cooperation.

COMPLIMENTS

When the therapist returns to the therapy room after consulting with his team behind the mirror or after having thought about the case by himself, he begins the intervention messages with a series of compliments. These are statements from the therapist and/or team about what the client has said that is useful, effective, good, or fun. This helps to promote client-therapist fit and thus cooperation on the task at hand.

With some frequency, the compliments (in the first session) will include statements about the difficulty of achieving the chosen goal and some statements, based on the exceptions, about the progress toward the goal and the general viability of the goal. In later sessions, the main focus of the compliments will often be on the progress toward the goal.

"Fit" is a qualitative term that involves the client-therapist relationship, the pathway the interview takes, the goal(s), all of which help to make the present salient to the future and thus give sense to the therapy situation.

SET OF ALL KNOWN TASKS

Pattern analysis (de Shazer, 1978b, 1979a, 1979b, 1982b, 1985; Dolan, 1985; O'Hanlon, 1987) of cases suggests the situationally specific nature of therapeutic interventions. These ways of looking at the therapeutic endeavor allow for the transferability of tasks — or the pattern of task — between widely varying problems or symptoms or complaints. That is, if Case Q's description includes a spontaneous exception and so did Cases D and J, then a task that involves predictions will probably be useful in Case Q since it was effective in Cases D and J. Of course the task might have to be tailored to fit (a variation), but the pattern of the task (the theme) could be the same or at least based on the same principles.

It is here (on the map) that the therapist's experience and reading come into play. Any task that any therapist has found useful might be transfered and modified to fit the particular pattern(s) involved in the specific clinical situation.

SET OF RULES TO HELP DESIGN
OR INVENT NEW TASKS

Goals help to define how therapist and client alike can know that the problem is solved. In a very real sense, goals are the target that therapist and client shoot for and, at least for brief therapists, the tasks are like arrows. That is, tasks are designed to get to the goal like an arrow is designed to get to its target. Like an arrow leaving the bow, once a task is assigned it either reaches the target or it does not, although the therapist and client might be satisfied if it is merely going toward the goal (i.e., increased change talk). The therapist is aiming for any spot on the target whereas the archer is aiming for a bull's eye.

Once a good arrow is designed it needs to be properly put in place before it can leave the bow. Similarly, intervention design can be seen to actually begin during the conversation between the therapist and the client, and the therapist needs to pave the way for the task assignment during the interview itself by focusing on change talk. Searching for exceptions and defining how to know when the problem is solved are two of the techniques designed to elicit and promote change talk. The effectiveness of a well designed task depends, at least in part, on how logical and reasonable it seems to the client, and this logic is built up through talking about change during the session.

General Guidelines

(1) Note what sort of things the clients do that is good, useful, and effective.
(2) Note *differences* between what happens when any exceptions occur and what happens when the complaint happens. Promote the former.
(3) When possible, extract step-by-step descriptions of any exceptions.
   (a) Find out what is working, and/or
   (b) find out what has worked, and/or
   (c) find out what might work, then
   (d) prescribe the easiest.
   If some aspects of the exception (or of the complaint) are sort of random, then
   (e) include something arbitrary or make allowances for randomness in the task.

(4) When necessary, *extract* step-by-step descriptions of the complaint.

(5) Note *differences* between any hypothetical solutions and the complaint.

(6) Imagine a *solved* version of the problematic situation by:
   (a) making *exceptions* into the rule,
   (b) changing the *location* of the complaint pattern,
   (c) changing who is *involved* in the complaint pattern,
   (d) changing the *order of the steps* involved,
   (e) adding a *new element* or step to the complaint pattern,
   (f) increasing the *duration* of the pattern,
   (g) introducing *arbitrary* starting and stopping,
   (h) increasing the *frequency* of the pattern,
   (i) changing the *modality* of the problematic behavior.

(7) Decide what will fit for the complainant/customer, i.e., which task, based on which variable (a through i) will make sense to the particular client. Which one will the complainant most likely accept? Which one will the customer most likely perform?

For instance: If a couple has a joint complaint, give them a joint, cooperative task. If only one member of a couple presents the complaint like a customer, give the "customer" a task that involves doing something and the other person an observation task.

The following chapters will use case examples to illustrate the various pathways shown on the central map of this theory of solution. Sectional maps from the central map will highlight the pathways to help distinguish between the various options.

7

DECONSTRUCTION[1]: A WAY OF DEVELOPING FOCUS

The constructivist philosophers (Watzlawick, 1984) have suggested that reality is more what we make of it than what it might really be. The principles of reframing and the constructivist ideas behind it, i.e.,

> to change the conceptual and/or emotional setting or viewpoint in relation to which a situation is experienced and to place it in another frame which fits the "facts" of the same concrete situation equally well or even better, and thereby changes its entire meaning (Watzlawick, Weakland and Fisch, 1974, p. 95)

have long been part of the brief therapy mores and play an important role in many schools of family therapy.

According to Goffman (1974), frames are definitions of a situation that "are built up in accordance with principles of

---

[1]The term "deconstruction" as used here is meant to fit within a "radical constructivist" view (von Glasersfeld, 1984). It is not necessarily meant to fit within the scope of "deconstruction" in literary criticism as Derrida (1981) uses the term and the use of similar terms, i.e., "undecidables" is coincidental. Any similarities in use and meaning is an unplanned bonus.

organization which govern events – at least social ones – and our subjective involvement in them" (p. 10). Frames are the "rules" by which we construct our reality and different rules might apply in different situations. Reframing, then, is a process that involves helping the client transform his or her "rules" for developing meaning out of a particular problematic situation.

Sometimes clients' frames, or how they define what it is that is going on, seem rather global. Of course, any frame can be described as if it at least helps to determine the person's behavior. But in some cases clients frame their difficulties and problems in such a way that the frames become "facts of life." For example, someone might blame all his difficulties on the sun's rising in the east. This may seem absurd to an observer, but it could lead the owner of the frame to unusual and bizarre behavior. As long as that premise helps to determine how the person sees things and, therefore, how the person behaves, then beneficial differences are unlikely. But once a person comes to *doubt* that premise, then an expectation of change is created (de Shazer, 1985) and different behaviors and different ideas are at least possible, perhaps likely.

DECONSTRUCTING

In the majority of cases the exceptions and their relationship to the goal provide therapist and client with something to focus on during the course of therapy. Any particular interview can readily be focused on the task at hand and both can easily know when the problem is solved in a satisfactory way. But when a global frame is involved, such focus is difficult because anything and everything falls within therapy's target.

Developing some doubt about global frames involves a process that can best be called *deconstructing the frame*. During the interview, first as the therapist helps the client search for exceptions, and then as the therapist helps the client imagine a future without the complaint, the therapist is implicitly breaking down the frame into smaller and smaller pieces. As it becomes clearer and clearer that a global frame is involved, the therapist helps the client break it down further into its component parts. The purpose of breaking the frame down is threefold:

(1) The therapist is showing his acceptance of the client just as he is by listening closely and carefully asking questions,

(2) the therapist is attempting to introduce some doubt about the global frame, and

(3) the therapist is searching for a piece of the frame's construction upon which a solution can be built.

The confusion technique is a version of this process designed to lead the client to demand clarity and specificity. More generally, the deconstruction process is designed to lead the therapy situation to some *undecidable*, some point at which the entire logic of the global frame would call for thoughts, feelings, or behaviors that are outside of those currently used by the client. When global frames are involved, the therapist searches for some point within the client's logic that he or she has not followed through to a logical conclusion or, when the complaint is overly focused on some narrow or singular area of life, the therapist searches for something outside the narrow confines of the complaint as the client describes it.

More formally, the purpose of the therapist and client working together to deconstruct a global frame and/or a complaint is to produce an *undecidable*, a focal point upon which to build a solution. An *undecidable* functions as a disorganizing intervention which undermines or at least pokes holes through the client's global frame. Frequently this is disorienting and confusing for the client because he cannot decide what is going on based on his usual logic. The therapist is searching for some point, any point, in the client's logical system that is *alogical*, a point that will bring down the whole of the problematic construction. Of course, any simple undecidable point or element can be seen as related to the system-as-a-whole — it is something complex. Building on an undecidable allows for the development of more useful frames.

Difficult Cases

Frames color how their owner (creator) behaves toward other people and therefore how they behave toward him. Mead (1934) suggested that a person's self-image is based on how that person sees other people seeing him. Thus if a therapist frames a case as a "difficult" one, he or she is on the way to behaving toward the client in ways deemed appropriate for dealing with difficult cases. Frequently, people who behave in strange ways and/or who have bizarre ideas are experienced in dealing with therapists who think of them as "difficult" cases. Thus if the client sees the therapist treating him as a "difficult case," then the client will come to see himself as a "difficult case," and consequently a difficult case develops. The frame "difficult case" becomes a self-fulfilling prophecy. Ideas about reframing and self-image suggest, however, that when the therapist frames things differently and responds differently from what the client expects, the client will then come to see himself differently. Thus the client's frame may be placed in doubt and more useful behavior might follow.

At first glance, the idea of helping the client develop some doubt about how he frames situations may seem absurdly small and simple given "traditional" ideas about "difficult cases." However, general system theory has long held as axiomatic the idea that a difference or change in one part of a system will lead to repercussions (and transformations) in other parts of the system. This simple idea forms the foundation of brief therapy (Weakland, Fisch, Watzlawick, and Bodin, 1974; de Shazer, et al., 1986) in general.

Since global frames can be seen as if they are "rules" for defining life in general rather than concrete situations, reframing any specific situation will not give the framer any news of difference. Even when the reframe is accepted, it will not be a difference that makes a difference because the global frame will still apply to everything else. For instance, if a child is seen as a liar, one particular truth-telling event will usually not shift the framers' perception of the child: He will still be a liar. Or if a child is seen as "bad," eliminating one bad behavior will have little or no effect on his parents and how they frame their experience with the child.

In cases in which the client presents a global frame, he and the therapist are unlikely to be successful in the search for exceptions. Even when the therapist and/or team clearly see something as a potentially useful exception, this will not prove meaningful to the client.

The cases discussed in this chapter are usually described as "difficult cases." A word of caution: "Difficult cases" is simply a name for the frame therapists often use to define what it is that is going on in certain cases. There are many reasons for this "difficult case" ascription, but it boils down to this: strange ideas and bizarre behavior seem to demand complicated descriptions and elaborate explanatory meta-phors, i.e., a "difficult case" results. Following from this is the not very useful idea that a complex description *means* there is a complex reality underneath and therefore, therapy must be equally complicated. This idea is based on a break-down of the distinction between "map" and "territory." Simply, a map is not the territory. A description is not the prob-lem it describes.

Any map only needs to be "good enough" to be useful – to get the users where they want to go. For instance, to go from Illinois to California, passing through Denver, all you need is a map that says: Find and follow Interstate 80 West. You do not need to know that you will pass through Omaha on the way and you need not know about the rivers and mountains. Of course you might miss a lot of interesting things if your travels are built on following this rough map, but you will get where you want to.

The following section map is used to describe the cases in

this chapter. Again, the sections of the central map that are not illustrated by these cases have been eliminated.

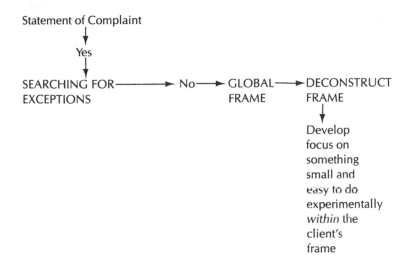

The questions about these cases, derived from the theory:

(1) Is there a complaint?
Yes
(2) Is there an exception?
No

(This response eliminates all the sections to do with deliberate and spontaneous exceptions.)

(3) Is there a hypothetical solution?
No
(4) Is the complaint concrete and specific?
No
(5) Is the complaint vague or confused?
No
Then, begin deconstructing the complaint.

One needs to be careful in drawing conclusions from single case studies or even from the study of several cases illustrating the same point: they may just be exceptions to some unknown general rule or they may even be flukes. But they may be important: they may be anomalies that lead to some new theoretical understanding and/or new intervention techniques.

A unique event, such as described in the following case example, provides a point of departure. Although rapid transformation is not unusual in the practice of brief therapy, the simplicity of the approach to what is traditionally seen as a "difficult case" suggested that this was unexplored territory.

CASE EXAMPLE FIVE

Therapist: "I bet you that most people don't believe you're really the devil."

A 28-year-old man, Mr. F, claimed to be the devil: the serpent from the garden of Eden. (His medical records indicated that this was not a new idea. He had been making this claim since he was eight years old.) He therefore claimed to be the prime cause of all the evil in the universe.

At this point he was in a halfway house after having been in the hospital. He had not held a job for more than a week in the previous four years. Now he wanted a job and did not want to go back to the family farm since he had been alienated from his family for four or five years. Throughout the previous 20 years he had been in and out of therapy, in and out of hospitals, and frequently on medication. He wanted to break that pattern but saw little hope of that, but saw the first step as getting off medications and then out of the halfway house.

Mr. F readily agreed that most people did not believe he was really the devil. I suggested that if I were in his shoes this lack of belief would really piss me off. He agreed. Again, if I were in his shoes, I thought that I would want to prove it to all those doubters. He agreed that he wanted to prove it to people, particularly his family. I wondered how he was going to go about it. He said that the ultimate evil was nuclear holocaust: This would be the proof. I agreed that the holocaust was certainly evil enough to qualify as the ultimate evil.

However, I saw one problem. Again, if I were in his shoes, I thought that I would want people to grovel and to acknowledge the truth: that he was indeed the devil and the cause of all the evil in the universe. But, after the holocaust, there would be nobody there to acknowledge this truth. What good would it do?

Throughout this statement (which is only summarized above), Mr. F sat motionless, eyes wide open and unblinking. I then stood up, and so did he. We shook hands and scheduled the next appointment.

Obviously, arguing with Mr. F about his claim to be the serpent had not worked during the previous 20 years, and so I needed to make sure that I did not let that happen. I needed to accept his premise, his global frame. The conversation flowed naturally until I was able to develop something "wrong" about the conclusions following from his beliefs or how he framed his situation. In this way some doubt could be introduced.

During the next two sessions he talked exclusively about the steps he was taking to get out of the halfway house. With his physician's approval, he had gradually stopped his medications and was beginning to look for a job. He had applied for several and had enlisted the help of an agency. During the two weeks following the first session he had not felt "weird" at all (and he had not behaved "weird" according to the halfway house staff). There was no devil talk during either session.

Within a few weeks he found a job as a live-in companion to a elderly man. He was responsible for shopping, cooking, laundry, cleaning, and giving the employer a bath, helping him dress, and driving him. The only contact during this period was over the phone when he reported doing well. During the third month of this job, he called on a Monday for an appointment which could not be scheduled until Friday of the same week.

He said that he had originally called to get some medication, but that he no longer felt that need. On the previous Saturday, he had started to feel "weird" again, thinking about being the devil, etc. But he had to continue giving his boss a bath. So, he gave him his bath. Then, even though feeling "weird," he had to help him dress, fix the evening meal, do dishes and clean up. By the time he was finished with his chores, he was so tired he went to bed and fell asleep immediately.

The next morning, though still feeling weird, he had to help the man dress, drive him to church and then drive him home again. Grocery shopping had to be done, the house had to be cleaned, dinner cooked, etc. He continued his work while continuing to feel weird. By Monday he was simply tired, but no longer felt weird.

Previously when he had had attacks like this, he ended up in the hospital by the end of the first day. He would have been heavily medicated and would have lost his job since getting out of the hospital had always taken four to six weeks. But this time he just forced himself to continue working. On Sunday he had made an interesting discovery: He was not the source of all evil; God was. In fact, as he saw it, he had actually been protecting the universe from the evil God. He went into this scenario in detail and at great length. At the end of the session we shook hands, and I said: "Hang in there. Lord knows we need all the protection we can get." He smiled broadly and said nothing.

He was not seen in therapy again. When, over the course of a year, he made payments on his bill, he reported the following: He continued to hold his job and felt good about it. Over the previous four years, his visits to his family had all ended up with hospitalizations. However, since getting this job, he visited his family twice and neither time did he find himself feeling weird. He had taken no medication and had not been in the hospital. He also reported feeling "somewhat weird" now and then but he ignored it and continued doing what he was doing.

CASE EXAMPLE SIX

The apparent success of the approach in the above case led to the following approach of attempting to *deconstruct* a global frame by helping the client develop doubts about how he is framing his entire life situation. At this point a tentative rule was followed:

> *The process of deconstruction involves accepting the people's frame as logical up to the point where it produces troublesome behaviors. Explore the total situation until an undecidable or potential focal point develops. Then, question the logic of the behavior within the person's frame.*

Therapist: "How come the CIA sent such incompetent killers?"

Therapy began with Mr. G, a Vietnam vet and a former CIA operative, complaining about the plot against him. The plotters had recently escalated by having someone accidentally ram into the rear-end of his new van for the second time in six weeks. Mrs. G came to therapy complaining about Mr. G's having recently purchased a side-arm which he had carried in the car. She was afraid for her life and the lives of their two children. She had notified the local police.

He tried to reassure her about her safety as well as the children's, but his violent attacks on her in the middle of the night prompted doubts. She saw his behavior and fears as "getting worse, day-by-day." She was concerned when he took apart the TV and the phone looking for bugs, and when he took sentry duty around the house through much of the night. She did not mind his not sleeping and he usually did nothing during his patrols to disturb her or the children until the previous four nights when he carried a loaded automatic.

He defended himself as protecting her, the children, himself, and their home. Since he had worked for the CIA, he knew how they worked and that was why he took apart the TV, the phone, radios and hunted for bugs throughout the house. He knew that the accident with the car was not an accident: it was, in reality, an aborted attempt on his life.

Throughout the previous 18 months his wife had tried to logically convince him that he was imagining things: The CIA was not out to get him and the accidents were simply accidents. However, her approach did not work. All Mr. G did was talk less to her in general and keep quiet about the plot while thinking more and more about it. Recently, in fact, he had begun to withdraw and was hardly talking to her at all about anything.

Being realistic and trying to talk him out of his beliefs had been his wife's approach, but that did not work and it is important for the therapist not to do something that has already not worked. Therefore, the first step is to accept Mr. G's beliefs at face value: behave as if there were a CIA plot against him. Then, think about what is *wrong* about the details of his description of the CIA's plot. Most simply, what is wrong with the details is that the two attempts on his life had failed miserably: The CIA had not even come close to killing him. How come? When the CIA plans to kill someone, they do it. Therefore, the question is: Why would the CIA send incompetent killers? What's wrong with the CIA?

Following this line of thought, I asked Mr. G, "How come the CIA sent such incompetent killers?" "Don't CIA operatives usually know what they are doing?" "If you wanted to kill someone in your situation, couldn't you do a better job?" "Wouldn't the guy already be dead?" "What's wrong with the CIA?"

He agreed that if he had wanted to kill someone like him, he would already be dead. He could not figure out why the

CIA had sent such incompetents and I asked him to think about this puzzle.

I then switched topics, offhandedly suggesting loaded guns were not a good way to protect his family. What if there were an accident and the gun went off and he accidentally killed one of his kids or his wife? This he did not want and he agreed to think about unloading the guns around the house.

Then, I asked to speak to Mrs. G alone for a minute or two. I told her that since pointing out logic to him had not worked, she ought to stop trying it. Repeated attempts to convince him that he was wrong would only make him think she is part of the plot and that she was trying to get him to let his guard down. In fact, she said, he had recently started accusing her of being in on the plot. I suggested that whenever she thought he was thinking about the plot, she should quietly get next to him and—without a word—give him a hug. She should not argue with him about the plot and she should not walk away when he withdrew.

He interpreted her disbelief as proof that she thought he was crazy. He also interpreted her "just letting him brood" as further proof that she did not believe that the CIA was after him. Therefore, if she avoided walking away from him when he was thinking but gave him a hug instead, since that is rather different behavior, there is some chance that he would interpret it as she no longer thinks he is crazy. This interpretation would be strengthened by her no longer arguing "logically" about the situation.

The process of deconstruction led to a focal point which stood some potential for globally reframing the whole situation. Mr. G's central premise (i.e., how he framed or defined what was going on) was that the CIA was after him. He had no question about that. By accepting that premise I was able to begin to introduce doubt by questioning the CIA's behavior and thus his central premise. Similarly, the suggestions to Mrs. G were intended to introduce doubt about his idea that she thought he was crazy. In both cases, doubts are essential to successful therapy because the client needs to "see through" the global frame he or she has given the situation in order to develop options.

I maintained my frame throughout the subsequent sessions. Whenever the topic of the CIA came up, I wondered about its incompetent operatives. He would share in this puzzle. I would then switch to wondering about what he had done that was good for him, and he would then describe his efforts to fix up their house so that they could sell it. After the fifth session, he dropped his ideas about the plot (or he at least stopped talking about it and stopped acting as if he believed in the plot's reality). Once in a while he still heard voices from the TV but now he knew they were not real and therefore he did not act on them.

Mrs. G reported following the suggestions and discovered that her husband was extremely responsive. When she resisted the urge to be logical or to walk away and hugged him instead, he would snap out of his "bad mood" and return to his tasks.

During the seventh session (three months after the first), he reported planning to go back to fulltime work since the house was now completely ready to sell. They reported increased team work and improvement in their sex life. (Six months later, he was still only talking about going back to fulltime work, but had not done anything about it. He continued to occasionally hear things over the TV but no longer paid attention to what was said. The marriage continues to go well.)

Once some doubts were introduced in session one, I focused on what they were each doing that was good individually and for their relationship. Once these activities were described, I encouraged them to do more of the same. That is, I concentrated on working with them to build a more satisfactory marriage based on what they did that was good for them (de Shazer, 1985).

Simply put, on one hand, "doubt" can be seen as a way of introducing a small difference, or an exception to the global frame, while, on the other hand, "hugs" can be seen as introducing a small step in the solution. As the hugs increased we talked more what they were doing that was good for them. As the doubt increased we talked about the CIA less and less. Hugs and doubts together allowed them to construct a more workable view of reality.

CONCLUSION

Of course, no approach always works. It seems that failures with "difficult cases" can often be associated with the therapist not accepting the client's complaint at face value, i.e., if I had either tried to talk him out of being the devil or to treat the (so-called) psychosis, rather than helping him get out of the half-way house, as he requested, then cooperation would have been very difficult and neither the therapist's nor the client's goals would have been met.

These cases suggest that reality is constructed out of some rather flimsy stuff, not concrete and stone. For therapists, this is good news. Even problems that are traditionally seen as "difficult" are subject to rapid transformation — under the right conditions:

(1) The client's frame of his situation seems to be global or all encompassing. The client considers the frame to be "a fact of life." This one central idea seems to determine many different behaviors, thoughts, feelings and perceptions in many different contexts.

(2) Previous therapists and other significant people have attempted to reasonably point out the error involved in this framing.

(3) Deconstruction involves the therapist's accepting the clients' frame as logical up to the point where it produces troublesome behaviors, thoughts, feelings, and perceptions.

(4) Deconstruction involves the therapist's exploring the client's situation, sometimes in great detail and at great length looking for a *focal point* or an *undecidable*.

(5) Once a focal point develops the therapist questions the logic of the behavior, thoughts, feelings, and perceptions *within* the client's frame.

(6) The therapist helps to get other people intimately involved with the client to behave *as if* they accepted the reality of the client's frame. This usually involves reversing typical behaviors.

(7) The therapist promotes whatever the client is doing that is useful, effective, good, and fun.

(8) The therapist attempts to find out when the frame was not in operation when the client and his significant others would have expected the frame to be in operation.

8

USING THE THEORY

The theory (Chapter 6) is meant to describe the alternate pathways that therapist-client interaction follow during therapy sessions. Each of the following case examples is preceded by the section of the central map that applies to the case.

How a therapist describes a case to himself early in the first session immediately constrains the range of possible solutions. This initial description and/or statement of complaint, though often vague, helps to determine where the search for exceptions begins. A "wrong" choice can lead to a decided lack of fit, a poor choice of tasks, and failure.

CASE EXAMPLE SEVEN

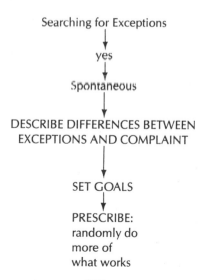

Searching for Exceptions

↓

yes

↓

Spontaneous

↓

DESCRIBE DIFFERENCES BETWEEN
EXCEPTIONS AND COMPLAINT

↓

SET GOALS

↓

PRESCRIBE:
randomly do
more of
what works

The following questions illustrate how we use this section of the central map.

(1) **Is there a complaint?**
Yes
(2) **Is there an exception?**
Yes
Describe difference(s) between complaint and exception(s).
(3) **Is it "deliberate"?**
No
Then, include allowance for randomness in any task assigned.
(4) **Is there a goal?**
Yes

Session 1

A young woman came to therapy complaining about feeling depressed all the time. The therapist, defining the complaint in much the same way, began to search for exceptions, i.e., times when the young woman was not depressed. Quite a few exceptions were found and clearly defined in behavioral terms. One of the young woman's ideas stood out: the various men in her life contributed to her feeling depressed. The complaint is, however, defined as having something to do with internal states.

The therapist gave the young woman a task built around paying attention to what was going on when the exception occurs and to notice what is different about those occasions.

Session 2

The young woman reported her observation in detail but said that things were not better. In fact, things were worse now than ever before. Doing the task had given her a new perspective on her situation. What she was really depressed about was her relationship with her boyfriend – nothing else. But giving up was "out of the question." She thought that he needed to change so that their relationship could be better.

She saw no possibility of his coming to therapy but she was interested in doing what she could to help him change.

```
BETTER?——▶ No ——▶ Check on
                    task performance——▶Yes——▶Deconstruct
                                                complaint
                                                pattern
                                                   │
                                                   ▼
                                                SELECT:
                                                One of all known
                                                tasks
```

The young woman had performed the task, but things were not better. However, by doing the task she was able to begin deconstructing the complaint, and therefore the complaint was narrowed down and redefined as "feeling depressed about a relationship with a young man." From this vantage point, the search for exceptions in the first session had failed: at no time was she not depressed about this particular phase of her life. It was confirmed in the second session that, other than in relationship to this young man, she was doing fine with her life.

The client's doing the task from session 1, including her report about the exceptions which was rich in detail, could lead the therapist to assuming that things are going well unless or until he asked about whether or not things were better.

This suggests a task focused on this problematic relationship including the idea that the young lady needs to *do something different* vis-à-vis the young man.

Session 3

She reported that things were better because she had taken the initiative and called her boyfriend about going to her office picnic (which he had previously refused to do). He again refused, saying that if she was going to nag him, he was done with her. She burst out crying; he hung up the phone. She had thought this would be the end of the world but the next day was not too bad. She remembered her report on her life, given in session two, and decided that maybe she would be OK. At this point "nothing could make me take him back." She went to the picnic alone and had a "decent" time.

The therapist, of course, had no idea what she might decide to do that was different and this episode and its results were a surprise. Since she was not confident that her world would not yet end, another task was given and another session set:

> *"Between now and next time, pay attention to what you do to overcome any urges you might have to feel depressed about the break-up."*

Session 4

She had rebuffed her ex-boyfriend's efforts to get back together which had pulled her out of the beginnings of another depression. She had also discovered that simply moving to a different room or getting out of the house or leaving her desk at work was enough to help her overcome any tendencies to feel depressed. At this point she thought that things were better enough, but scheduled a checkup for six weeks later.

Six weeks later she called instead of coming into the office. Although at times she felt lonely, she was not at all depressed and was more active doing things both by herself and with her girlfriends.

CASE EXAMPLE EIGHT

The best way to design a failure is to establish a poor definition of the complaint. This can be done in many ways, and the following is only suggestive and not exhaustive. Tomorrow we will find another way.

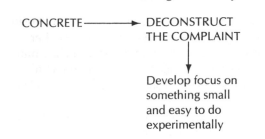

CONCRETE ⟶ DECONSTRUCT
THE COMPLAINT

⬇

Develop focus on
something small
and easy to do
experimentally

Session 1

"All we want is for our son to be a normal, productive adult," said the mother of a 25-year-old who had not held a job for more than six weeks during the preceding six years.

Of course, any mother will want that for her child, but it is not a goal for therapy. To meet that goal, therapy would have to continue until the young man becomes old and retires or dies and that might take 50 years. If the therapist accepts that as a goal, therapy will fail.

Mother's complaint is that her son is not normal, a conclusion based on the following:

(1) He does not have a real job where he has to go at the same time every day and put in 40 hours per week;
(2) he drinks too much too often;
(3) he probably uses drugs (although tests previously given at a hospital showed otherwise);
(4) he sleeps too much;
(5) he had not had a real job in six years;
(6) his girlfriends are as bad or worse than he is.

All of this she blamed on her son's "poor self-image." Father pointed out that "Of course he has a poor-self image because he never has been successful at anything."

Two years previously, mother and father gave up on their son and threw him out of the house. This had not worked very well and at the end of six months the son threatened (according to father) or attempted (according to mother) suicide. Then the son returned home with their permission.

Thus the therapist attempted to negotiate, asking mother and father about "What will need to happen, what will he need to be doing that will say to you, 'the odds of his being a normal, productive adult are better than they were yesterday'?" Neither mother nor father was able to define what the signs would be, but the son—who wanted the same thing—suggested that his getting up on time and going to work every day would be some indication.

At this point, mother and father appeared to have a "complainant type" relationship with the therapist while the son was indicating that he was a "customer" who was ready and willing to do something about getting up on time so that he could work when work was available. This version of the complaint is better, but is still not good enough. Mother agreed it would be a "beginning" but it was not what she wanted. It was also not quite what the therapist wanted, since therapy would need to continue until the son retired.

So, the therapist asked the son "Once you are getting up on time and going to work, how will you know that the pattern is established? How will you know that the odds have increased on your continuing to be independent and productive?" He thought it would take five or six weeks. From the son's point of view, therapy could stop when he had gotten up and gone to work for six weeks in a row.

This version is far better, but still not quite good enough. For instance, if he misses one day in week five, does that mean the six week cycle starts over? For the son, "no," but for mother "yes." Mother could not agree to the idea that if he did not get fired for missing that day, then the count would not have to start over.

For the therapy team the goal "six weeks of getting up on time and going to work and not getting fired for missing work during that period" was good enough. Therefore, they suggested some techniques for helping him get up on time and asked mother and father to observe what differences it made.

"We suggest that you buy two more alarm clocks, which would give you three. Set one for the time you need to get up so that you can get to work on time, then set one for one hour earlier, and then the third for another hour earlier. Then, in the morning, when the first one goes off, you turn it off and have the pleasure of going back to sleep. Then, one hour later, again turn it off and have the pleasure of going back to sleep. When the third one goes, get up."

Session 2

Over the course of the next two weeks the son got up on time every day, often leaving for work before mother did. He had purchased the alarms, but only did the task for three days after which one was enough. Father reported that tensions were eased and conversation more frequent. Mother saw it as "an improvement" but thought that the change did not get at the real heart of the matter. She pointed out that her son had only done the task three times and, therefore, was not serious about solving even this problem. The son, however, felt better about work and about himself. He was willing to bet that he would continue to get up on time, now that he knew how, because he wanted to save enough money so that he could move out.

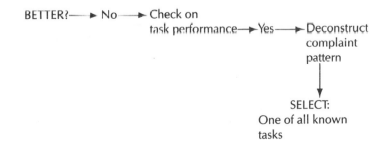

Although the son continued to go to work every day, mother and father – over the course of three more sessions – were not able to give this the significance that the son did.

Therefore, since from mother and father's perspective things continued to be "not better" for two sessions in a row, various attempts were made to deconstruct their complaint. Nothing the son did provided the parents with any doubts about how they viewed him.

BETTER?——▶ No ——▶ Second time here,
                               redesign complaint
                               or deconstruct
                               complaint pattern

At this point, the son saw the problem as solved and refused to continue in therapy.

Further attempts to deconstruct the situation, i.e., by reframing both their parenting and the son's "slow but sure approach" also failed. Mother and father, therefore, also refused to continue – since it was the son's problem – and were not satisfied with the results.

For mother her son's achieving his goal was not a difference that would make a difference. The son and the therapist and team were pleased, but since mother is not "more satisfied" then, for her, therapy failed. At follow-up, six months after the son is continuing to get up on time and get to work and had almost enough money to move out, mother is still not more satisfied even though dad is and she clearly said that therapy did not help her reach her goal.

What did mother want? Or, more importantly whatever she might have wanted, how would she ever know when she had it? In order to prevent this failure, the therapist would have had to be successful at deconstructing her global frame (my son is not normal). The son's reaching his goal was not enough to make this undecidable for her vis-á-vis this frame.

At this point, some rules for failure can be suggested:

(1) Have a poorly defined complaint.
(2) Have a poorly formed goal.
(3) Have a goal – no matter how well formed – that when achieved does not make a difference.

CASE EXAMPLE NINE

"I want us to get back together," and "so do I, but I am not ready yet" said the young couple who separated three weeks earlier.

It is easy for the therapist to assume that "getting back together" is a reasonable goal in this case. But it is poorly formed in several ways. First, the "I am not ready yet" needs to be clarified: the wife may be asking for a miracle to happen before she can be ready. Without that clarification, failure can be predicted. Second, just "getting back together" is not well enough defined to serve as a goal. If they get back together and nothing is different, then unhappiness is almost assured and another separation nearly inevitable. Therefore, the goal needs to be expressed in a different way, i.e., what needs to be different so that once back together things will be different *enough*? What needs to be different so that they can feel confident that another separation is not right around the corner?

The couple was unable to describe how they would know when it was time to get back together or what it would take for them to be successful once they got back together. They would just know that the time was right because it would feel right. She was unable to say how she would know when she was ready: she would just know.

For the therapist, one way to think about this is to frame the complaint as "we don't know how to know when to get back together." There are no exceptions to this complaint.

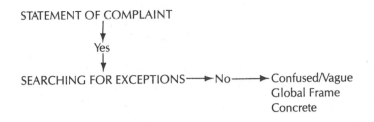

The following illustrates the use of this sectional map.

(1) Is there a complaint?
   Yes
(2) Is there an exception?
   No
(3) Is there a hypothetical solution?
   No
(4) Is the complaint vague and/or confused?
   Yes

This construction might lead the therapist to giving them some version of the formula first session task. Or, the complaint might be framed as "we want to get back together but we don't know how."

CONCRETE————▶ DECONSTRUCT
                THE COMPLAINT
                    │
                    ▼
                Develop focus on
                something small
                and easy to do
                experimentally

This construction would lead the therapist into giving them a task focused on helping them make a decision they will find satisfactory. However, their non-specific or non-behavioral descriptions suggest that re-structuring and/or deconstructing the complaint in the second session might be difficult.

When faced with a decision of this sort, the FFST is the more conservative and is to be preferred. This variation was given to them at the end of the session:

"Between now and next time we meet, I would like you to observe what happens between you that makes you think that the time to get back together is approaching.

"However, a word a caution: Getting back together before both of you know you are both really ready is most likely not to work out. The biggest danger is getting back together too soon."

But what looks like the best decision at the time can

prove, in the end, not to be useful. During the two-week interval before the second session, she had an impulse to move back in and did so. Within 24 hours, things were again a mess between them. He moved out and within 24 hours had seen a lawyer and filed for divorce. She was shocked, but knew, as she reported in a phone call, that she had acted unwisely. She still loved him but now he said "he feels betrayed and I have no idea why."

Two more rules for failure can now be suggested:

(4) Have an unclear goal.
(5) Have a concrete goal without knowing what is expected to happen as a consequence of meeting the goal.

CASE EXAMPLE TEN

SEARCHING FOR EXCEPTIONS————▶No
        ↓
HYPOTHETICAL
SOLUTION
        ↓
Describe differences between Hypo-
thetical Solution and Complaint
        ↓
SET GOALS
        ↓
PRESCRIBE:
Do easiest of
what might work

While brief therapy, in general, is a goal-oriented approach, our solution focused model demands knowing how therapists and clients alike, will know *when* the problem is solved. In fact, this question is the primary hub around which other questions revolve. If therapist and client have established measures of success, what the original complaint was does not matter. They can simply work on developing ways to meet the goals!

complainant?]	customer?
someone who has a complaint	someone who wants to do something about a complaint

At times, it can be very difficult to make the decision about whether any particular person is at any particular time developing more of a "complainant relationship" or more of a "customer relationship" with the therapist. Sometimes during the course of a single session the relationship can oscillate between the two.

Session 1

She said that she had been having severe "panic attacks" for about seven years and could not remember even one day when she had none. On the average, she had attacks twice daily during the entire seven years. Although she was sure there were infrequent days when she only had it once, she could not remember any one specifically. Each day, if she did not have an attack at 10:00 a.m., then it would be at 11:00, if not then at 12:00. The second one would be at 7:00 p.m., if not then at 8:00.

In response to the miracle question she listed the following as ways her life would be different:

(a) an increase in the number of meals eaten with other people;
(b) a return to graduate school;
(c) cooking and having people come to dinner;
(d) a new wardrobe;
(e) going out alone for pizza;
(f) visiting with mother who lives out of town;
(g) staying home alone watching TV; and

(h) having other people remark "Hey, you're looking good!"

She saw not having panic attacks as the pre-condition for these activities (a through h). With a clear description of goals like this the therapist can sometimes design tasks, with the client's assistance, that promote these behaviors (measures a through h) and not have to design tasks that focus on eliminating the "attacks."

However, when I asked "Suppose that we had something for you to do, which we were awfully sure would work, would you do it?" she said that she would have to know what it was before she could promise because she was "chicken" and wanted to do things slowly and carefully. This suggests that we have more of a "complainant" type relationship than a "customer" type and therefore a task based on the responses to the miracle question seems "too fast" for her.

CONCRETE⟶DECONSTRUCT
THE COMPLAINT
↓
Develop focus on
something small
and easy to do
experimentally

A decision needs to be reached and some small task seems the more conservative. Picking "introducing arbitrary starting and stopping" because of the clock-like regularity she described, the following task was designed:

"Since you decided you wanted to take a 'slow way' rather than a 'fast way,' I would like you to, between now and next time, should you feel an attack coming on, delay starting it by at least 5 minutes but not more than 15 minutes each time and observe what you do during this period."

Even minimal delay that was deliberate could lay the foundation for increasing delays. Even unsuccessful efforts would provide some constraints on a next step while successful efforts would increase the number of options. Importantly, the task was not designed to stop or prevent attacks per se. Rather, the task was designed to accidentally trigger an exception (at best) and to help make a decision between "complainant" and "customer." Like so many apparently behavioral tasks, there is also an implicit message: "You have control" which might allow her to see through her "I am helpless" frame.

Session 2

She reported that going for a walk was the one thing she found to help her delay starting, but she did that only a few times. In general, things were not better even though on one occasion she had walked downtown, met a friend and spontaneously went to lunch with her. She did not have even a mild attack: a first. This event encouraged her and she then started to do the task more often, but without any new exceptions. Furthermore, she was now "sick of being sick" and wanted to switch to "a faster way" although unwilling to switch to "the fastest way."

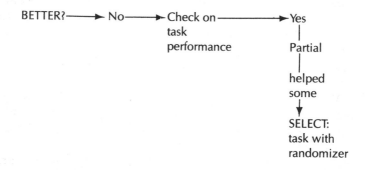

Things are not better but the task, when she did it, helped some. This indicates that a task needs to make room for her to make decisions about when to do it, any task at this point needs to include randomness as a possibility.

"Fast and slow ways," "faster and slower ways" can be

used as a measure of the complainant/customer's determination to do something. Picking a "faster way" suggests that the relationship in the second session likely falls more into the "customer" category.

"Here is a 'faster way,' but certainly not the 'fastest way.' Between now and next time, each night before going to bed, I want you to decide which of the eight things on the list would be the easiest for you to do the next day. Then, toss a coin: heads you'll do it, tails you won't. It's perfectly OK to do 'two out of three' with the coin toss should you want to. By the way, the current record is six heads or six tails in a row."

This gives her a lot of choices, some of which are easier than others. And the coin toss following the decision has the potential of saying "no" to something she picked that she also really wanted to do.

Sessions 3, 4, 5, 6

She only tossed the coin the evening after this session and was relieved that it came up "no." Over the course of four more sessions she reported that, each night she decided whether or not the next day would be a "do day" and picked from the growing list. By session 5, most days were "do days" on which she did not have attacks. In each session the task was the same: "You're headed in the right direction — keep doing it."

At the start of the sixth session, she reported tossing a coin to decide whether or not to keep the appointment which she no longer felt she needed. It had come up "no," but came anyway, just to have the fun of firing me.

Six weeks later, she called because the day before she had become afraid of having a "giant panic attack." She was afraid it was starting again. I asked, "So, what did you forget to do?" She thought about it for awhile and then said that she had, on the previous evening, forgotten to decide what she was going to do the next day.

Six months later she reported that attacks were history

although every so often she would forget to plan and then a fear of anxiety would develop. She had not yet returned to school nor had she visited her mother because she was still not confident enough.

DISCUSSION

In every case that a therapist sees there are perhaps millions of possible decisions to be made. As a rule of thumb, the most conservative is usually to be preferred. That is, when the question is "complainant or customer?" it is less risky to decide that a "complainant relationship" is developing and, therefore, an observational or thinking task is better. Being less cautious, i.e., giving a behavioral task within a "complainant relationship" might lead to "nonperformance" and potential troubles in the therapeutic relationship.

9

EXCEPTIONS: THE CONSTRUCTION OF SOLUTIONS

SECTION MAP FOR CASE EXAMPLES IN THIS CHAPTER

STATEMENT OF COMPLAINT

SEARCH FOR EXCEPTIONS?

YES

DELIBERATE ? SPONTANEOUS?

Describe differences between exceptions and complaint

SET GOALS

PRESCRIBE:
Do more of
what works

PRESCRIBE:
Randomly do
more of
what works

CASE EXAMPLE ELEVEN

   Miss B, 24 years old, came to therapy wanting to break
her cocaine addiction. She had been shooting coke into her
arm for 18 months, sometimes spending up to $1,000.00 a
night. In fact, she had discovered that she had spent more
for coke in the previous year than she had earned on her job.
At the start of the session she presented herself as helpless
with regard to coke. She saw no chance of quitting on her
own and was thinking about putting herself into a hospital.
In fact, what she really wanted was for me to use hypnosis
to make her hate coke. Violating a cardinal rule of doing
therapy, I am afraid to say I laughed at her, telling her that
was just a silly coke dream. She was not taken aback and
persisted: She wanted me to "make her stop," but again I
laughed at her and said I could not do that, only she could
do that! She stuck to her guns: It was her idea that she was
helpless and that her coke use was beyond her control.
   I was curious about her life "outside the realm of coke,"
but before I could ask about what she did when she did not
do coke, she told me that she had not had any coke for three
days—her longest period without in over a year. "But that
ain't nothing!" she said: she still craved coke. At this point,
simply not doing it was not enough. Miss B thought she also
had to stop craving it and therefore she dismissed these
three days as a fluke. However, I saw them as the start of
the solution—SOMETHING TO BE UTILIZED. From my
perspective, she knew how to solve the problem, but she did
not know she knew. So, I explored what she had done differently:

   (1) she unplugged her phone,
   (2) she refused to answer the door,
   (3) she came home, watched TV and went to bed early,
   (4) she worked on her rug hooking hobby, and
   (5) although she did not tell me about it at the time, she
       also turned over money management to her aunt who
       worked in the same office.

When I told her for the third time that these were exactly the kind of things she needed to continue doing, she agreed.

The Miracle Question

I then asked her: **Suppose that one night, while you were sleeping, there was a miracle and this problem was solved, even though you continued to like coke. What difference would that make?** Miss B thought that then she could handle things and would be able to say "no" to coke which is a reasonable goal. But, at this point she thought that would indeed take a miracle. She then told me about a major exception to her rule about being helpless in regard to coke: she had never stolen or sold her body to buy it.

I then asked her to **Suppose that we had some things for you to do which we were pretty damn sure would work, would you do them?** Without any hesitation she said "yes." After a long pause (giving her time to modify or retract her quickly given "yes"), I pointed out that they might be very very difficult things to do, but they would be possible and they would be legal and moral. She did not back out of her commitment.

Using the theory leads to the following:

(1) **Is there a complaint?**
    Yes
(2) **Is there an exception?**
    Yes
(3) **Is it deliberate?**
    Yes
    Describe differences between complaint and exception.
    Then the task should prescribe that the client does more of what is already working.
(4) **Is there a goal?**
    Yes

After an intermission, in addition to complimenting her on what she had done the previous three days and telling her to continue doing that, we suggested she pay attention to what she does WHEN she overcomes the urge to do coke.

This is a handy task, because it

(1) acknowledges that there will be urges;
(2) suggests that the client will overcome some of the urges;
(3) acknowledges that they might fail to overcome some urges;
(4) focuses the client on "doing something"; and
(5) suggests that the therapist expects the client to do something to overcome some urges.

Furthermore, it is transferable, i.e., "pay attention to what you do when you conquer the urge to act depressed or beat your husband, or suck your thumb" (de Shazer, 1985).

Since her parents were giving and loaning her money, fully aware that she used at least some of it for coke, we asked her to have her parents sign a statement that they would never loan or give her money until she and they were absolutely convinced that she would not use it for coke[1]. She did this and they agreed to sign it.

But how did I know what to do in this session? As I see it, the answer is simplicity itself. For three days in a row, the young woman had not done any coke. This is noticeably different behavior, particularly when she had presented herself as a helpless addict. This news of difference served as a red flag to indicate which of the potential pathways to use in helping her construct a solution.

I quickly became curious about what differences made this difference. Was it just chance and therefore difficult for

---

[1]As a "rule of thumb," efforts need to be made to help outsiders stop contributing to any problem. The statement is merely the easiest available. Should it fail, then a session or two with her parents is called for.

It can also be useful for the therapist to frame "drug, alcohol, and food abuse" as "money abuse," particularly when money is of concern to the client. It is also a less loaded way to frame things and can lessen the urge to consider these problems as somehow different from other problems.

her to repeat? Had she deliberately done something in an attempt to stop which, by accident, had worked? The distinction between her experiencing a chance event and her finding something that worked helped me decide what to do next. She had deliberately done something different in regard to cocaine three days before our first session. At least for these three days she had not been helpless in the face of her so-called addiction. Here was an interesting exception to the rules of her complaint.

But it was more than chance exception, it was a *deliberate* difference that she initiated prior to coming to therapy. She was able to describe some of the ways these three days were different from the days on which she had used coke and the descriptions were good enough that she would be able to deliberately continue them. At first she had little confidence in her solution, so I knew that I needed to do something that pointed out this success and encouraged her to continue doing something that was already working. Like many people with a problem, she thought that her solution would prove, in the end, not to be good enough. And certainly without her mentioning these three days to me, the difference might have gone unnoticed and could well have become just another miscarried solution. Therefore, my task became helping her make this difference into a difference that made a difference thus resolving the complaint.

In at least one more respect, her three days without coke can serve as a lens for looking at "exceptions." Although some exceptions are "spontaneous" (see below), others involve deliberate efforts on the client's part which will lead to the therapist's thinking and his teammates saying behind the mirror that "this problem's already solved!"

Importantly for my knowing what to do, four of the five behaviors that she described as different did not involve the cooperation of anybody else. Thus, her continuing to promote and elaborate these differences is greatly simplified. If other people's cooperation had been necessary, her job might have been made more difficult because they might not have done their share.

The *miracle question* has become a standard way at BFTC to check out the client's expectations and set goals. In this case Miss B gave a adequate reaction: She would begin to say "no" to cocaine. As is frequently the case, the client's response to this question serves as a goal statement for therapy.

Since I had turned down doing something, (using hypnosis to make her stop or to make her stop wanting coke), and since she had deliberately done something toward stopping coke and agreed that she needed to continue doing those things, it seemed important to confirm with her that she and I had agreed it was her job to do things. By the end of the interview, prior to the consulting break, she had agreed to do what my team and I told her to do. I left it wide open just in case, but knew that in part, our instructions to her would be to continue doing what she had been doing for three days, thus stressing the importance of what she had already done toward saying "no" to coke.

Session 2

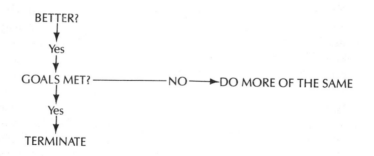

Questions at the start of the second session (and subsequent sessions).

(1) Does the client say things are better?
Yes
(2) Does the client say that the goals are met?

No

Then, the next intervention should be similar to the previous one since it is working.

When the client says that the goal is met, it is time to terminate or at least discuss terminating. Termination may need to be delayed until the client has confidence in the solution.

Therapist: So, how are things?

Client: Great!

Therapist: What the hell are you doing right?

Client: Huh?

Therapist: What the hell are you doing right?

Client: I'm not doing coke.

Therapist: That's 17 days?

Client: 17 days and counting. I'm marking them off on my calender.

This exchange opened the second session. She appeared shocked by my asking her what the hell she was doing right, perhaps thinking that is not a way for a professional to behave, or perhaps nobody had ever before accused her of doing something right. Regardless, she told me.

She had found it difficult to keep track of urges and what she did to overcome them, but had quickly invented a way: When she was at home and became aware of an urge to do coke, she moved to a different room and started to work on her rug making hobby. She continued the same behaviors but added house cleaning, laundry, and even grocery shopping to the behaviors she performed that helped her continue coke free. She also began to think differently about coke. Where previously if the urge to do coke came on, all she could do was think about the "high" and ignore the "down" which followed; she now thought about the "down" part which inevitably followed. Not having the downs was important to her and so she thought she had a better chance of continuing coke free than she did two weeks before.

Although skeptical about having found her own solution, she nonetheless thought her chances of slipping, of using coke in the immediate future, were 50/50, which she saw as more hopeful than two weeks earlier. The team members behind the mirror on the whole agreed with her; half thinking that any slipping would happen sooner rather than later, half thinking it would be later rather than sooner. I disagreed with the whole group. I thought the chances of her slipping in the immediate future, i.e., between the second and third sessions, were very slim simply because she had invented the whole treatment approach. Nothing she was doing was foreign to her, it all came from her repertoire. This disagreement was presented to her at the end of the session along with the suggestion that she continue doing what was working for her.

Again, how to know what to do in the second session is simplicity itself. She was continuing to behave in ways she did not associate with coke, in ways that she in fact now associated with not doing coke. Therefore, one of BFTC's rules of thumb apply: **Once you know what works, do more of it.** The client was following that rule and therefore so should the therapist. When the client reports that "things are better," then the therapist only needs to help the client recognize what is working and help her figure out ways to do more of the same type of things.

Over the course of four more sessions (in three months) she found numerous things to do to overcome the urges, none of which I suggested. Throughout therapy, all of our interventions simply utilized what she was already doing and what she invented. By the final session (the sixth), six months after the first, her bet on her own success climbed from 50/50 to 80/20 in her favor. She doubted if these odds would ever be different. Once again utilizing something she had done that had proved effective, I suggested that she probably could raise the odds to 99/1 by simply promising herself that she could have all the coke she wanted as long as she sold her body to pay for it or she stole to pay for it. She smiled and agreed. Eighteen months later she was still coke free.

THE INFLUENCE OF MILTON H. ERICKSON

From the beginning, my work has been based on the principles I abstracted from Erickson's many papers. As I see it, my work and the work of my colleagues of BFTC continues to use Erickson's work as a point of departure. Interestingly, after years of using hypnosis or trance based methods in my practice (de Shazer, 1978, 1979), more recent work (since 1982) has been done without any deliberate efforts to induce trance. Yet I see my work now as more hypnotic and as further expanding the work Erickson initiated.

For instance, I see the consulting break we take during the session as almost like a trance induction since the client, while waiting, seems to become more receptive to what the therapist says when he or she returns to the room. This state is heightened and enhanced through the messages we construct. These messages start with complimentary comments from the therapist and team about what the client is doing that is "right," "good," and "effective" — continuing to build a "yes set" (begun during the interview phase of the session) which fosters the client's expectancy — before we give the client our therapeutic suggestions. While delivering these compliments, we frequently see trance like behaviors, i.e., "unconscious head nods," shifts in breathing rates, the assumption of a more relaxed sitting posture, etc. And clients tend to do some version of the task when the "yes set" has been established.

Utilization

When Erickson talked about "utilization" he meant many things. Sometimes he defined it as "utilizing" the problematic behaviors, thoughts, and feelings as part of a therapeutic solution. One aspect of this meaning has come to be described as a "symptom prescription," a tool which certainly can be useful in some situations.

"Symptom prescription" is not the only thing Erickson meant by "utilization." He had a second definition that is more general, "'utilizing' a patient's own mental processes in ways that are outside his usual range of intentional or voluntary control" (Erickson, Rossi, and Rossi, 1976, p. 19). My definition is related and yet different, at least in point of emphasis. From my perspective, "utilization" involves "utilizing" whatever the client does that is somehow "right," "useful," "effective," "good," or "fun" for the purpose of developing a solution.

Basically, I think we therapists have gotten hung up on "problems" and how to solve them. If you listen to therapists, they frequently talk about "the treatment of phobias," or "the treatment of bed wetters," or "the treatment of conflictual couples," or "the treatment of families," or "the treatment of couples," or "the treatment of individuals." Those therapists who talk this way seem to think that these cases or problems are all somehow different and that the problem and/or the number of people involved determines the treatment.

As we continue to study how solutions develop, we are concluding that there are more similarities between the treatment of phobias and the treatment of wet beds and the treatment of conflictual couples than there are differences. And I am not sure that these differences make any difference! I suspect that many people are as shocked by that idea as I was at first. But I hope it does not keep them up nights like it did me. But it is the only conclusion my team and I could come to that fit our experience.

CASE EXAMPLE TWELVE

A charming 56-year-old woman, Mrs. C, came to therapy because her paraplegic husband had been increasingly irritated at her distraction when he needed her. She was "absent minded" because she was spending time arguing with the voices in her head. Then, of course, she would not hear her husband when he called. The voices had been with her for many years, but she was afraid they were getting worse. She had not been hospitalized for over thirteen years and wanted to prevent that from happening again. Realizing that she might "always" have the voices, she wanted to stop arguing with them because she needed to pay attention to her husband.

Mrs. C. thought that she was arguing more and more with her voices and nothing she tried would make them go away. It surprised her when, early in the first session, I began to explore the times when she did not hear the voices, or did not pay attention to them, or did not argue with them even though she paid attention to what they said. She was only vaguely aware of times when she did not hear the voices or did not argue with them, but agreed to keep a detailed log for two weeks, even though she thought I should know more about the voices and what they said and perhaps even be interested in "why" she had voices.

I asked her to carefully note what she was doing

(1) when she did not hear the voices,
(2) when she did not pay attention to them,
(3) when she did not argue with them, and
(4) when she knew her husband knew that she was not paying attention to them.

For me, it was a question of "What was Mrs. C doing that was effective, useful, or good during those periods when the voices did not irritate or distract her?" Once these "spontaneous" exceptions could be described in behavioral terms, she could be encouraged to do more of the same or similar things. Hearing the voices of people who were not there was simply accepted as part of the way Mrs. C viewed the world. For me, it was not a matter of trying to stop the voices but rather to increase the times or the proportion of time when she was not bothered by them.

In the second session (two weeks later), Mrs. C reported that she rarely argued with the voices before noon. During this period she was busy doing housework and taking care of her husband. She also discovered that by not arguing with the voices, they would sometimes be silent for the period she was busy; yet the moment she sat down she found herself arguing with them. She also discovered that she did not argue with them while the visiting nurse made her daily visit to her husband. We explored in detail what she did when she was "busy." Once these details were known, I simply suggested that Mrs. C do more of these activities. She agreed.

In the third session, Mrs. C reported that she had been able not to argue at all before 5:00 p.m. throughout the two week interval. She was busier and felt better. I again simply suggested that she continue to do more of what worked for her, and she agreed.

By the fifth session (two months after the third), Mrs. C reported that the voices had diminished as she argued with them less and less frequently and Mr. C's complaints had diminished in both frequency and intensity as well.

One year later, Mrs. C reported that she still had the voices in her head, but they caused her little trouble.

The goals of the therapy (helping to reduce Mr. C's complaints and helping Mrs. C argue less with the voices) were met simply through building on the exceptions to the times when she argued with the voices. The voices were accepted at face value and no attempt was made to eliminate them.

Alternate, More Complicated Constructions

Mrs. C's situation could have been described in many different ways. For instance, the voices could have been seen as an attempted solution. The voices were most active when she was least busy caring for her husband. Therefore, one could have suspected that the voices solved the problem of her appearing to be willing to nurse her husband while, in fact, she found this to be a burden. Mrs. C was in a no-win position: (1) either she cared for her husband *willingly*, without voices, or (2) she cared for her husband because she *had to* in order to quiet the voices.

The voices could have been thought of as serving a homeostatic function in the marriage: (1) keeping Mrs. C from leaving the marriage which suggests that without the voices there would be no marriage, or (2) helping her get her needs met as well through her "illness."

In addition to the systemic descriptions or explanatory metaphors, various intrapsychic ones might be suggested. However, the point is that any explanatory metaphor is more complicated than simply taking the complaint at face value: Mrs. C had nagging voices with which she wanted to stop arguing. Simply, this goal could be met with just some different behavior. Any or all of these explanatory metaphors might be useful in designing a more complicated therapeutic approach should the simplest one fail, but importantly, any or all of these explanatory metaphors might lead the therapist to miss the simplest available approach. Thinking that complicated maps necessarily represent complicated territory is seductively easy given the usefulness of these maps in some contexts.

CASE EXAMPLE THIRTEEN

Mr and Mrs D brought their 9 year old son and their 7 year old daughter to therapy with them. The parents' primary complaint involved the daughter's temper tantrums and a secondary complaint involved the boy's poor memory. Tantrums had been frequent, sometimes two per day, up until the day of the phone call setting up the appointment. Then, for three days in a row, there had been no tantrums! As dad put it, it was like having your toothache go away as soon as you called the dentist.

I quickly began to explore what was different on those days without any tantrums. Brother and sister had been involved, really involved in playing a game together and the parents were involved in their own household tasks. The game had gone without conflict and thus the parents were able to relax and enjoy themselves without having to arbitrate and/or punish misbehavior. However, these conditions were not that unusual, i.e., the children frequently played games together and there were frequently times when the parents would be involved in household tasks. As far as anyone could see, these tantrum free days were simply flukes.

After complimenting the family members on each one's ability to describe things and on their obvious caring, we asked them to each secretly predict, every day before the daughter's bedtime, whether the next day would be tantrum free. The following day, before they made their next predictions, they were to account for the accuracy or inaccuracy of their predictions.

But What to Do?

Since there were exceptions, helping the family do more of whatever was involved in these differences becomes the focus of the interview. But, unlike Case Example Eleven where the differences were deliberate, in this case, as well as in Case Example Twelve, the differences were unplanned or spontaneous. This is the primary difference between the case examples.

The family and I were unable to describe what differences had made the difference on the three tantrum free days. However, something was clearly different about those days. But what? Had mother done something different? Father? Brother? Or the girl herself? If these days were really chance events, then repeating whatever was different is practically impossible. However, when behavioral differences can be described, then the chance differences can be performed deliberately. The task was designed to help us find out what *anybody* did differently on days without tantrums.

Of course that there were these three tantrum free days means that a solution has been found even though neither the family members nor the therapist know what it is or how to describe it. The family members, once always expecting tantrums, can now start changing their expectations and thus a solution is in process.

In the second session it became clear that temper tantrums could be aborted when the parent chose to ignore or walk away from the opportunities to engage in disputes about what they wanted the girl to do. Although nobody could predict temper free days, they found that after some fuss and perhaps some tears, the girl would eventually follow the directions. For the first time mother consistently used this technique and tantrums were fewer than normal, although it was not a temper free week.

After complimenting them again on their observational skills and on their persistence, we suggested that they continue to ignore any tantrums that might begin but, if one did begin before they had a chance to ignore it, then they should simply Do Something Different, perhaps something like walking away.

Although no differences were noted between days with tantrums and days without, it became clear that ignoring the tantrums made a difference, then doing more ignoring could be given as a task. At this point it is not known whether or not ignoring will be enough to handle the tantrums in a way that is satisfactory to the family. Neither therapist nor family members have enough experience with ignoring to have confidence in that as the most useful approach.

Mr. and Mrs. D had found something that made things better and therefore the intervention simply suggested that they do more of the same, i.e., ignoring, since it was working. Now that some difference has been noticed, the family needs to amplify that difference; this then might lead to a satisfactory solution.

CASE EXAMPLE FOURTEEN

Session 1

Mrs. Z brought her husband to therapy because she wanted him to stop abusing alcohol. Mr. Z said he did not abuse it, and he did not want to stop drinking. As it turned out, he had promised her many times to stop drinking. He would then have just one when visiting his folks who ran a tavern, but that always seemed to lead to more because he felt bad for having broken the promise, which he had not really wanted to make in the first place. One of the first things I did was suggest that he no longer make that promise. He agreed. I explored with him what he did when he was not drinking. I explored with her what she saw him doing when he was not drinking. And I explored what she did when he was not drinking.

From this first session it is clear that there were times when he did not drink and that both of their behaviors, separately and collectively, were positively influenced. However, there was not enough time in the first session to go into details about any non-problematic patterns. Therefore,

> *we asked them each to individually keep records about what they did separately and what they did together during the coming week when he was not drinking.*

This task indirectly prescribes the exception's pattern. That is, in order to do the task, he has to not drink. Directly suggesting that he not drink would only continue the wife's unsuccessful approach.

Session 2

During the week, Mr. Z had not had a single drink, but before he described his observations, he set the stage by comparing what happened with what usually happened when he did drink. As he put it, his drinking changed her tremendously. She was like a different person as soon as she even suspected that he had been drinking. When he was not drinking, she waited on him hand and foot, made his favorite meals, scrubbed his back, reminded him of his household tasks, bought him little gifts, packed his lunch, initiated sex, etc. Although this was a list from just one week, there had been a period of two years when she behaved like this while he was not drinking. Mrs. Z reported that he had done some long delayed tasks without her having to remind him, and that he had given her spontaneous hugs. Both described this week as wonderful, but she was afraid that it might be a fluke since she was not at all confident that he would not drink again. He said that the minute she even suspected he had had a drink, she stopped these behaviors, withdrew, and bitched about everything. This was enough to "drive anyone to drink." Then, when she knew he had had a drink, she would go to her mother's. Then he was lonely and drank more. Eventually, he would promise, she would return and things would go well until . . .

Mr. Z made it perfectly clear that he had little or no interest in stopping drinking at her request. If and when he were to decide to stop drinking, then he would. He wanted her to "get off his back," and declared his intention of not coming to further therapy even though I had made it clear that I would not tell him to stop drinking. She decided that she would come on her own to work on coping with a situation which she did not want, i.e., continuing a marriage with the constant threat of his again drinking too much. Her continuing in therapy was O.K. with him because "it really is her problem, not mine."

This week without drinking and the two year period without drinking confirmed the potential usefulness of the exceptions. At one point, the exception had, in fact, been the rule. Therefore, I simply suggested that

> *since you found out what works for you, I can only suggest that you continue doing what you did this past week.*

Except for not drinking, his part in the exception pattern was not very clear. Both of them were easily able to describe her part and quick to notice the differences between the abuse pattern and the exceptions pattern. Thus I could readily work with her to promote a solution through doing more of what worked in the previous week. His participation so far had been useful and his continued participation might have also proved useful, but it is not essential for developing a solution.

Session 3 (two weeks later)

Mr. Z continued not drinking and she had not even sus-pected that he drank. But she was worried. She knew that her approach had not worked and she also knew that she wanted this marriage to continue and to be successful. I suggested to her that next time she suspected he had been drinking, she was to pretend she did not suspect and to carry on as if things were fine. She was to go out of her way to serve a favorite meal and then to take him to a movie and initiate sex afterwards—all normal behaviors. She was to observe his reactions and then to observe the consequences.

That is, I suggested that she continue the exception pat-tern regardless of what really happened. The idea in mind was that her doing her exceptions behavior would promote his responding in kind.

Since Mrs. Z was unwilling to pretend things were normal if she discovered that he actually had been drinking, I sug-gested that she think about what she was going to do differ-ently if she came home and found out that he had been drinking before she got home. I suggested that she think about what he would LEAST expect her to do, and then do it. Immediately, she said that he would least expect her to take him drinking. We both laughed at this imagined event even though she found it "a repugnant idea."

When it came to actually discovering his drinking, Mrs. Z lost confidence in the "pretending" approach even though it had thus far been successful "beyond her wildest imagina-tion."

Sessions 4 and 5

Over the course of the next few months, she pretended a few times and—whether he had been drinking or not is not known—it did not escalate and she did not go to her moth-er's. Then one day she came home and saw his army buddy's car in front of the house. She KNEW that this meant drink-ing, so she went to the neighborhood shop and bought two six-packs of the most expensive foreign beer she could find. Then she went home and placed the beer on the kitchen table where they had been sitting. She had been right, he had been drinking some. She sat down and insisted that her husband drink the beer she bought him as a surprise – sticking to her normal behavior of bringing a surprise now and then. He was shocked. His buddy, sensing trouble in the air, wisely left, and she continued to insist that as long as he was going to drink he should drink her beer. He would not. One year later, the two six-packs were still in the refrigerator and he had not been drinking.

When she suspected that he had been drinking, she substituted *her normal* behaviors and the drinking did not escalate. And when she knew he had been drinking, she again substituted *normal* behaviors, i.e., bringing him a surprise (the foreign beer). And the drinking did not escalate. He values her surprises and so, if he is going to drink again, he will have to drink her surprise beer *first* because if he drinks other stuff, he would be rejecting her surprise and this would probably break up their marriage. This he does not want. Neither of them might realize how central her surprises and his responses to her surprises are to the marriage and I would not tell them. As of one year after our final session, he does not abuse alcohol, and she continues to give him surprises – which he values.

Of course, one cannot generalize from this case (involving abuse) to other cases (involving abuse), i.e., that other wives can perform the same "surprise behaviors" and pretend in the same way because, if for no other reason, not all marriages depend on her surprising and pleasing him and on his responding so well. Cases are not alike in that way.

The solution involves her doing something different from the usual complaint behaviors; *and* these so-called "different" behaviors are really normal for her, they are already part of her repertoire; *and* from his point of view, she is behaving in ways associated with good times, and so he has to respond with "good times behavior" since he values the marriage as much as she does. That is, the intervention was designed to

UTILIZE their non-complaint behaviors within the context of resolving the complaint.

If the marriage had been on the rocks, and he was no longer responding to her surprises during good times, then this approach probably would not have worked at all. That is, the system has to be connected in order for systemic or interactional changes to be effective.

THE *SAME* BUT *DIFFERENT*

Of course, no approach always works. It seems that failures in this solution-focused approach can often be associated with the therapist's not accepting the client's complaint at face value, i.e., if the therapist had either tried to eliminate Mrs. C's voices or to treat the (so-called) psychosis, rather than helping her stop arguing with them, as she requested, then cooperation would have been very difficult and neither the therapist's nor Mrs. C's goals would have been met.

Based on the kind of simple ideas I described above, I have been called "the most minimal of minimalists" (Brewster, 1985). This was probably not meant as a compliment, but I certainly take it as a profound one. From a minimalist's perspective, it is best to assume that a wet bed is simply a wet bed, teeth-grinding is teeth-grinding, voices are voices and nothing more. We have more complex explanatory metaphors available upon which to build a treatment approach should the first, most minimal approach fail.

If you want to get from point A to point B, but know no details of the terrain in between, the best thing to do is assume that you can go from A to B by following a straight line. If that assumption proves faulty and you run into huge mountains, then you need to look for a pass that is as close as possible to your original straight line. As William of Ockham might say, never introduce complex descriptions when simple ones will do.

For many therapists—those who see themselves as oriented toward family therapy as well as those who see themselves as oriented toward individual therapy — it might be difficult to conceive of all four case examples as being more alike than different. After all, Eleven involves an individual who sees herself as addicted to cocaine, Twelve involves auditory hallucinations, Thirteen involves a family dealing with the daughter's too frequent temper tantrums, and Fourteen involves a couple dealing with alcohol abuse. Within this model however, the cases are alike because all four clients describe exceptions. In each case, the primary emphasis is on describing what they did differently during the exceptional period; the therapist then prescribes more of what the client has found that works. This process is essentially alike in all four cases despite the presence of four people in Case Thirteen, two in Case Fourteen, one in Cases Eleven and Twelve. Number of individuals is not a complicating factor.

10

AN UNUSUAL CASE THAT FOLLOWS THE RULES

CASE EXAMPLE FIFTEEN

STATEMENT OF COMPLAINT
↓
SEARCH FOR EXCEPTIONS?
↓
Yes
↓
SPONTANEOUS?
↓
Describe differences between
Exceptions and complaint
↓
SET GOALS
↓
PRESCRIBE:
Randomly do
more of
what works

A 27-year-old woman, Mrs. E, came to therapy claiming to be a "dependent personality" who abused food and alcohol. I wondered if she abused both at the same time, and she said "No, I either abuse food (overeating and vomiting) or alcohol and sometimes other drugs." She never abused both at the same time. I was surprised and asked her how she decided which to abuse. She did not decide: it all depended on how she felt. If she could only solve one of these at a time, I wondered which one she wanted to work on first but, since she saw both abuses as "symptoms" of one underlying problem, she thought she needed to solve that underlying problem and thus both symptoms would be cured.

At the beginning of the session, Mrs. E described herself as having one big problem: food and alcohol abuse which was due to being a "dependent personality." She described this as follows:

COMPLAINT PATTERN A

(1) X (possible trigger)	◄───────────────────	
(2) Feeling bad		T
(3) Abuse food or booze		i
(4) Feeling bad		m
(5) Abuse continues		e
(6) Abuse stops		↑
(7) Return to "normal"	─────────────────────►	↑

This is not a very useful construction because the food abuse and the alcohol abuse are described as "the same thing" or, at least, variations of the same thing.

Some models of therapy (Watzlawick, Weakland and Fisch, 1974; Haley, 1976; de Shazer, 1982a) are based on the idea that the so-called "symptom" is a problematic step or element of a problematic pattern and therefore, the problem can be solved by eliminating that step or by changing some other step in the sequence so that a new pattern or detour forms.

A problem solving therapist might explore this sequence in detail, looking for details of each step along the way. Then, based on the idea that any transformation in a system means that the rest of the system has to respond, he or she might suggest that the client vary any one of the steps. When all goes well—as it frequently does—the client reports a difference in that sequence and reports that the "symptom," i.e., either the food abuse or the alcohol abuse or both is absent and an alternate version of the pattern develops.

However, since the food abuse is distinct from the alcohol abuse, I began to destructure the complaint so that there were two distinct problems before looking for exceptions since, once it is seen as two problems, then two different sets of exceptions might be developed.

COMPLAINT PATTERN A′   COMPLAINT PATTERN A″

1. X   X′
2. Feeling bad a′   Feeling bad a″
3. Abuse food   Abuse alcohol
4. Feeling bad a′   Feeling bad a″
5. Food abuse continues   Alcohol abuse continues
6. Abuse stops   Abuse stops
7. Return to normal   Return to normal

NORMAL DAYS PATTERN NON-A

She had been abusing food or alcohol for ten years and had been in and out of treatment (inpatient and outpatient) many times. Once again she was seeking therapy because her marriage had broken up and she wanted to either fix the marriage or herself so that she could "have a decent relationship with a man."

At the start of the first session, she described herself as

either abusing food or abusing alcohol but, as it turned out, we were able to describe three kinds of patterns:

(1) the good days pattern — usually two to seven in a row;

(2) bad days pattern, type A′: she would feel bad one day and KNOW, by the way she felt bad, that she would binge and vomit on the next day and several days following; and

(3) bad days pattern, type A″: she would feel bad and KNOW that she felt bad in a particular way that would lead to abusing booze for up to seven days in a row.

Rather than trying to either stop the problematic pattern (A or A′ and A″) or to vary any of the steps in the sequence, solutions can be built on getting the non-problematic patterns (*NON*-A) to happen with greater frequency. Thus the client is not asked to stop doing something (x) or to do something new but rather she is asked to "force" a normal pattern. Since the symptom is not a step in any *NON*-A pattern, it is less likely to recur. That is, the problematic pattern (A or A′ and A″) is not either stopped or transformed deliberately. Rather, it can be seen as if "pushed aside" through deliberate non-use. The problematic pattern can be allowed to wither away rather than be cut off.

Since we knew least about the details of the good days cycle (*NON*-A) and since she was in a good days cycle, I asked her to begin developing a catalogue of what she did during this cycle and to observe what she did when she overcame any urges toward bad days of either pattern.

The search for exceptions resulted in the idea that the "bad days pattern A″" was an exception to the "bad days pattern A′." Of course this meant that the "bad days pattern A′" was an exception to the "bad days pattern A″." Furthermore, not only were the bad days pattern each other's exception; the "good days pattern" was an exception to both bad day patterns.

Session 2

    She reported that she had had no urges to overcome dur-
ing the week between sessions but she had begun to develop
a catalogue of "good days behaviors and feelings." On the
good days she took care of herself, eating well, exercising,
visiting friends, going to church if it was a Sunday, calling
her parents long distance, etc.
    This she compared with her bad days, when she did not
do these things. Somehow she could tell one type of bad day
from the other. Although she could not define it so that I
could understand, she knew. These two types of abuse had
led to the break-up of her marriage. He left her because he
said that he was "not able to help her." He had said everything he tried only seemed to make things worse. They both
said they still loved each other, but refused to see each other:
each for the good of the other. Since it was working, I gave
her the same task at the end of the second session and the
third session was scheduled for two weeks following.

Session 3

    As the session began, she reported that the good days
continued: she had 30 in a row. She thought it was a miracle:
"Sometimes things do change overnight." I was not so sure.
Once again, I asked her to continue doing what was working, but also suggested that caution was appropriate since
there was no way to prove the absence of the two bad days
patterns.

Session 4

    This session coincided with a down day, of type A: she
knew that the next day she was going to binge on food. And
she really did not want to do that! So she agreed to do
whatever I told her, even before she knew what it was, just
so she did not have to go through another binge.
    After an intermission, I told her that she had two options:

(1) she could get up the next day and behave as she normally did during a good cycle; or,

(2) since she knew a food abuse cycle was coming, she should start drinking EVEN THOUGH SHE DID NOT FEEL LIKE IT. And, the next time she thought a booze abuse cycle was coming, she had to abuse food instead.

She looked shocked, but agreed that she had agreed.

For the purposes of this intervention, the alcohol abuse pattern and the good days pattern were both seen as exceptions to the food abuse pattern. In both choices she is asked to substitute a different "normal" pattern that at that time is "wrong" since she felt bad in a way that meant food abuse. Both the good days pattern and the alcohol pattern are different from the food abuse pattern which is the current complaint. Thus, either pattern performed at this point could prompt the development of a satisfactory solution.

Session 5

A week later, she reported that she got up the next day craving chocolate cake, but went out and bought some beer instead. She brought it home and sat there staring at it and shaking for three hours, then called her parents. Then she went to her exercise class and by noon she had forgotten her urge to binge.

The intervention which led to solution is built on something the client is already doing that works for her in day-to-day life. Since this behavior is already familiar to her, it is easy for her to cooperate with my task.

Sessions 6 and 7

Over the next six months she repeated pretending to have a good day about once a month. At that point, she described good days and "less good days," but no "bad days of either type."

The KEY is not in the details. Not every case can be solved by getting the client to blindly promise to do something "wrong." It is not the ordeal of promising to do the wrong bad thing that counts here. In the problematic situation, she did something different. What she did differently was to UTILIZE her non-complaint behaviors within the context of the complaint. Buying beer, calling her parents, going to exercise are ALL behaviors from non-food abuse days.

Of course, finding out what the client does that can be utilized to build a solution involves eliciting the right kind of talk during the session. If you do not ask about exceptions and successes, the client will not tell you. After all, what they are concerned about is the problem which drove them to seeking therapy. But, as Erickson said, "they don't know what the problem is." Therapists do not know either and we cannot know. All both clients and therapists can know is how to know when the problem is solved and, my conclusion at this time is, that when the problem is solved things will be much as they are now when the problem is not happening. Things will stop being "the same damn thing over and over" and revert to being "one damn thing after another."

DIFFERENT BUT THE SAME

(1) Complaint = Food Abuse

(2) Exceptions = Alcohol Abuse and Good Days

Spontaneous

Differences: When in good day pattern or in alcohol pattern, there is no food abuse

Goal: Increase the number and frequency of the good day pattern resulting in the absence of the abusing patterns. This would lead to better relationship with parents; restoration of marriage and/or building of a viable relationship with some mate.

↓

PRESCRIBE: Do more of what works = booze in food abuse pattern and/or food in booze abuse pattern and/or good days in either or both abuse patterns

Although one of the exceptions (alcohol abuse) is part of the original global complaint, it is also an exception to the *de-structured* complaint (alcohol abuse is separate and distinct from food abuse). However, this difference makes little or no difference in the pathway that led to solution. It is simply based on using non-complaint (non-food abuse) behavior within the context of the complaint, i.e., the food abuse complaint. Although this case, on the surface, appears radically different from those in previous chapters in terms of solution development, it is nonetheless the same in terms of both theory and method.

It is clear for this example that if Mrs. E had abused both food and alcohol at the same time, then each would not have been the other's exceptions. This means that some other exceptions would have had to be used to prompt a solution. This radical distinction between the two abuse patterns is what led to this unique intervention that clearly follows the simple rule: build the solution out of material from outside the patterns of the complaint.

11

VAGUE COMPLAINT, VAGUE GOALS, VAGUE SOLUTION

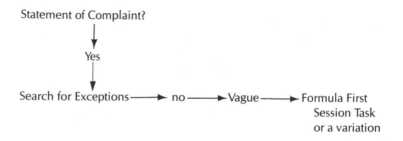

The purpose of the therapist and client working together to deconstruct a global frame is to produce an *undecidable*, but when the complaint is vague the situation has already reached that point. An *undecidable* functions to disorganize or undermine how a situation is understood, perhaps leading to significant disagreement about what is going on. This is disorienting and confusing for the client and the therapist because they cannot decide what is going on and, more importantly, nobody can decide how they will know when the problem is solved.

CASE EXAMPLE SIXTEEN

Session 1

Mr. and Mrs. W came to therapy when Mr. W came to the realization that "the kick" had gone out of their marriage. He

160

was not sure that he wanted to remain in the marriage and he was not sure that he wanted to break up the marriage. Simply, he did not know "which end was up."

As far as Mrs. W was concerned, nothing was different. During the preceding six months, which Mr. W described as "flat," she saw things as pretty well consistent with how they had always been since the honeymoon was over ten years ago. Day-to-day life was filled with normal ups and downs, and during those six months she had not been able to read any signs of trouble. This confused her because she had continued to see signs that things were OK and now she had come to doubt her own perceptions.

Neither Mr. nor Mrs. W were able to describe any differences in his behavior which might have served as a clue to the fact that something was wrong. As far as Mr. W was concerned, he had just started to feel "flat." He continued to behave normally and was not surprised that neither his wife nor his children were able to tell that something was wrong.

Since Mr. W had been behaving normally, Mrs. W thought that things were normal, but his telling her that things were wrong left her with doubts about her perception of the marriage and of him. Since Mr. W behaved normally but inside he felt flat, he also did not know what was going on.

"How will you know when the problem is solved?" Neither Mr. nor Mrs. W were able to define what a solution would look like because nothing "on the surface" was wrong. Of course, this meant that their children, friends, co-workers also would be unable to know when the problem was solved. Mr. W would know the problem is solved when he "felt right again," but Mrs. W had no way to know this except if he told her. But even his telling her that things were alright would not define a solution for her because there would be no confirming signs.

At this point, Mr. W, Mrs. W, and I all shared in the indeterminance of the clinical situation. The problem is vague, the solution is indeterminable, and Mr. W could not find any times in the preceding six months when he felt O.K. about the situation. The whole situation was confused or undecidable and therefore I continued to explore, looking for times when Mr. W knew things were OK that Mrs. W knew that he knew things were OK.

Prior to the previous two years they both were sure that things had been OK. However, most of the things they enjoyed doing together they were continuing to do. It was only the kick that was missing and only Mr. W would know when the spark was re-ignited.

In an attempt to build some measure of success, I asked several scaling questions: "On a scale from 10 to zero, with 10 being you want this marriage very much and 0 being it doesn't make any difference either way, where would you place yourself today?" Mrs. W gave it a 8, while Mr. gave it a 6. "With 10 being as confident as humanly possible and 0 being that you wouldn't give it a snowball's chance in hell, what would you say the chances are that you two will still be together two years from now?" Mrs. W gave it a 9 and Mr. a 7. "With 10 being the most kick you can reasonably expect in a 15-year-old marriage and 0 being absolutely none, where would you rate it today?" Mr. W gave it a 2 and Mrs. gave it an 8.

Once a scale is set up, there is at least a potential way to measure progress and perhaps solution. Subjective measurements are suitable for measuring subjective feeling states although behavioral differences would be more accessible to Mrs. W and other people. However, I need to accept this as undecidable and to remember that the solution might be just as indeterminate to me and Mrs. W. At this point further efforts to be concrete and to clarify the situation will not fit for Mr. and Mrs. W and could indicate to them that I was not listening or was finding fault with them. Therefore, I need to accept this lack of clarity and respond with an intervention that has a similar undecidable quality but with some sort of difference in point of view.

"I am confused, but that's OK. In a certain sense, you are paying me to be confused, because that means that I do not see things the same way you do and therefore the problem can be solved. I am impressed with how well you both described things that are difficult to describe and that, even though things are difficult between you, nonetheless, you are both committed to keeping it working on a day-to-day basis.

To help us figure things out, between now and next time, pay attention to what happens that indicates and/or confirms that there's hope for the relationship."

When things are as confused or ill-defined as they are with Mr. and Mrs. W, then a task which is wide open to many possible interpretations is quite appropriate. This task, in fact, is simply a version of the Formula First Session Task which is adapted to this situation in which behavioral signs or the meanings attached to them are undecidable. Perhaps a change in feeling can be attached to some behavior which would make things more clear.

Session 2 (One week later)

Better?——▸ no ——▸ Check on
                         task performance ——▸ yes ——▸ DECONSTRUCT
                                                                     COMPLAINT
                                                                      PATTERN

                                                                      |
                                                                      ▼

                                                                      SELECT:
                                                                      Pattern
                                                                      Interruption
                                                                      Task

Both Mr. and Mrs. W reported that the interval between sessions had been decent. In fact, both had a good time when they went out and each had perceived that the other had had a good time. However, they were both sure that nothing had happened that either confirmed or indicated that there was hope for the relationship. Things were not better, and they were not worse, but things were "better" in one way because it had not gotten worse in the way both had expected it to get worse: they had not had any big blow-ups.

As a rule of thumb, things are either "better" or they are "not better" (i.e., the same or worse), but for Mr. and Mrs. W and me, this was undecidable. Therefore, it is best to consider things as "not better" and to do something different rather than continue on the same path.

Mr. and Mrs. W had continued to attempt to figure out the problem and had attempted to break it down into its smallest components, but they had learned nothing in this process except that their normal problem-solving approaches had not worked. In fact, they were surprised that they had not yelled and screamed at each other because yelling and screaming had triggered resolution of various difficulties they had had over the years. However, neither of them felt the urge to yell at the other and, therefore, they did not.

Yelling and screaming at each other had proved to be a useful problem solving tool for Mr. and Mrs. W when they had problems between them before. Perhaps not yelling and screaming at each other was preventing them from solving this problem! Their not yelling and screaming, when that approach had normally led to resolution, suggested that I had misunderstood: perhaps Mr. and Mrs. W had constructed a global frame, i.e., "our marriage is falling apart" rather than the confused or vague situation that seemed clear in the first session. Since things are not "better," this is a distinct possibility. If so, then a possible focal point had developed: according to their logic, since there is a problem between them, they should be yelling and screaming, but they are not. Perhaps a task including yelling and screaming would be appropriate.

Alternately, this apparent clarity could be seen as the appropriate response to the wide open construction of the first session's message. If so, then the yelling and screaming task might also be appropriate and apparently logical to both Mr. and Mrs. W.

Even this potential focal point is, however, undecidable at this time which suggests that the situation remains as indeterminate as before and, therefore, the intervention should again be open to various interpretations.

Mr. and Mrs. W were clearly puzzled. Everywhere they looked to try and make sense of the problem had led to a dead end. They just wanted to get on with it: they were tired of dealing with the problem and not having fun, except for the one time when they had gone out together. As Mr. W put it, when the problem is solved, things will be the same, except that they will be spontaneous rather than routine.

Things were "not better" and the previous task seemed to be of no particular help. This suggests that the task in this session might be usefully focused on interrupting the pattern of the complaint in order to start a new pattern. On the other hand, the yelling and screaming suggests a potential focal point which in turn suggests a task that includes yelling and screaming since that is the approach that Mr. and Mrs. W have found successful in the past.

However, which of the two tasks to use seems undecidable. Rather than putting this in an "either/or frame," and arbitrarily picking one task over the other, a "both/and frame" which involves putting the two tasks together would produce some potentially useful interpretations.

"It seems clear that the basic structure of a workable marriage is firmly in place, but that the "kick" is missing. Thus even good times that are good for both are not quite good enough. Here's a couple of ideas that might give your marriage a kick in the right place:

"(1) Shut up! about the problem. If it were a problem that could have been solved by talking about it, by breaking it down into pieces, you two would have done it by now. There is no sense of continuing to do something that isn't working.

"(2) Since you have found that yelling and screaming frequently triggered a resolution to difficulties between you, perhaps that's what you need to do this time. Since this hasn't happened spontaneously, perhaps forcing something that has worked before will prove useful now.

"Two times per week, in the next two weeks, toss a coin to see who gets to go first. The winner gets to yell and scream about anything at the other for an uninterrupted 10 minutes. The loser only has to pretend to listen. Then the loser gets then 10 minutes to yell and scream – about anything. It doesn't have to relate to the winner's turn at all.

"Then, a 10-minute period of silence.

"Then another coin toss to decide whether to go another round or not.

"Then, if the coin says "no" to another round or after the second silent 10 minutes, the two of you go do something physical together."

Session 3 (Two weeks later)

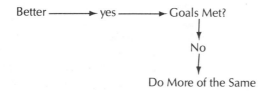

Both Mr. and Mrs. W were smiling as the session began. I asked: "Are things better?" Both said "yes," giving the two weeks an 8 on a 10-point scale. They reported that telling them to "Shut up" had been a very useful suggestion and that they enjoyed the joint physical activities without bothering with the yelling and screaming. Other than no longer discussing the problem, they did not see themselves as having done anything different except, perhaps, they did more physical things together. They could not see how this could have triggered the improvement. Both did, nonetheless, think that things were more of a kick or were more spontaneous.

Things are "better" and they both agree about the degree to which "things" are better. At this point the focus of the session can switch to finding out if things are "better enough" and finding out how confident they are about the *continuation* of this improvement.

Mr. and Mrs. W selected the parts of the tasks they thought might be useful and chose not to do the structured fight. (This suggests that the vagueness of the situation was a more salient view than the possible "global frame" around the marital interaction pattern.) Not talking about the problem and having more physical activities seemed useful and different enough to help them head toward solution. Regardless of task performance, the fact that they both reported that things were "better" is enough to inform the therapy system that solution involves them doing more of the same, whatever it is that they are doing. Solution will be found when Mr. and Mrs. W both rate the interval between sessions as "good enough" and both are rather confident that this "good enough" is likely to continue.

Both Mr. and Mrs. W thought that things were clearly headed in the right direction and, should it continue, it would lead to things being at least good enough. Neither of them were convinced it would last. They could not think of anything they could do to increase the likelihood of its lasting and the only thing they saw that might inhibit its lasting was going on an upcoming vacation together.

I fully agreed that they should continue to do what they were doing and that they were probably right not to be overconfident about things. No matter what, there will be good days and bad days. It was only important that they continue to do what they were doing that worked for them.

Session 4 (Four weeks later)

Better ⟶ yes ⟶ Goals Met? ⟶ yes— ▶ Terminate

Things continued to go fine for them, including the vacation period. They had not made the mistake of thinking it should be a second honeymoon and it turned out fine. They were convinced that somehow they had solved the problem even if they did not know how they did it. The only thing they saw that might get in their way in the immediate future were debates and/or conflicts about how to handle their younger child.

I suggested that each morning they should toss a coin to

decide who would be in charge of any difficulties that might come up with the child. The other one was just to observe the results.

Session 5 (Four weeks later)

Mr. and Mrs. W reported faithfully tossing the coin each morning and the only time anything happened they both felt relief that it was clear who was going to deal with it. This period had also served to increase their confidence in their solution. They felt that their married life was richer and both had a lot of confidence that these improvements would continue. Neither of them were, however, sure about what had happened to first make things stale and then to make things "better than ever before."

They decided to stop therapy at that point. We shook hands, wished each other luck and walked out of the office within less than 15 minutes.

DISCUSSION

When the therapy session itself is vague, with ill-defined problems and ill-defined solutions, everything that takes place is undecidable including improvements and worsenings. For therapists who assume that measurable goals are important, so that the difference between failure and success can be known, vague situations can be problematic. Attempts at clarity lead to more confusion but, importantly, attempts at adding more confusion or confusion of a different kind frequently lead to more clarity. However, the shifts from clarity to confusion are often frequent, sometimes shifting back and forth during the course of a single conversation.

It can be tempting to perceive this lack of clarity, focus, and direction as indicative of a "difficult case" and these cases can be constructed into difficult cases if the therapist does not fully accept the confusion or vagueness as a useful and necessary aspect of the total situation. That is, the confusion or whatever makes a situation undecidable can be utilized therapeutically providing that the therapist has confidence that the client(s) will eventually know when the problem is solved, and thus a more satisfactory life can develop. Of course the way of knowing a solution has been arrived at might be as undecidable as the original complaint, but even that can be useful when the client(s) have confidence that the solution is likely to continue into the future. Vagueness is problematic only when it leads to significant disagreement about what is going on. Without this disagreement, the situation is just indeterminate or potentially vague which perhaps holds for any interpersonal, interactive situation.

12

SPONTANEITY, UNPREDICTABILITY, SOLUTION

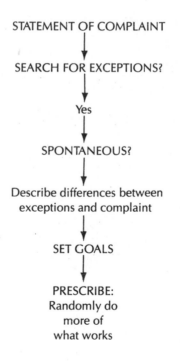

STATEMENT OF COMPLAINT

↓

SEARCH FOR EXCEPTIONS?

↓

Yes

↓

SPONTANEOUS?

↓

Describe differences between
exceptions and complaint

↓

SET GOALS

↓

PRESCRIBE:
Randomly do
more of
what works

CASE EXAMPLE SEVENTEEN[1]

Mr. H, a 25-year-old man, came to therapy complaining that "I have been depressed all my life." I asked him how he knew that he was depressed. Mr. H felt dissatisfied with his job performance, his friendships, his marriage, his relationship with his family, etc. Nothing seemed OK to him and, furthermore, nothing ever did. He could recollect no time in his life when he had not felt depressed.

I asked him, "So, since you've felt that way all your life, how do you know you are depressed and not normal?" Well, Mr. H then remembered "occasional 'up days'" as how he knew that he was depressed and not normal. But he pooh-poohed these days as meaningless. These up-days were simply chance events which did not shift his idea at all about having been depressed all his life.

Having found out that there were occasional, spontaneous exceptions the next task is to help Mr. H identify the differences between "up-days" and "down-days" in such a way that he can do more of whatever it is that works on those "up-days."

On "up-days," when he got up, Mr. H looked forward to the day, was organized at work, was more likely to play basketball, tennis, or golf. He thought he was more friendly and outgoing at work, enjoyed reading and even enjoyed doing housework and would go out after work for a couple of beers.

To further define the differences between "up-days" and "down-days," I asked Mr. H how his wife would know the difference without his having to say a word. Typically, he told me about the "down" side first. He saw her seeing him with a cold and distant look in his eye, but on "up-days" she saw him smiling more and talking more with her. Clearly, he saw other people as knowing the difference between a "down" Mr. H and an "up" Mr. H.

---

[1]The therapy in this case was done without a team.

As the interview continued, a clear picture of the difference between "up-days" and "down-days" developed. However, Mr. H continued to see the "up-days" as flukes or chance
events over which he had no control: It was not a difference
that made a difference. The picture was black and white:
"up-days" were clearly distinct from "down-days." To break
down that distinction and to assist in goal setting, I used a
variation of the scaling technique which I have found useful
in cases where the person describes himself or herself as
feeling depressed.

"On a scale from 10 (the worst your depressed feelings
have ever been) to 0 (you are either not feeling depressed or
the depressed feelings are completely out of awareness),
where would you place yourself right now? Mr. H thought
awhile and then rated himself at 5 or 6, the five simply
because today he was doing something about it, i.e., beginning therapy. He rated the previous evening at 8 and the
week's average as 7.

"What about the most recent "up-day"? This had been the
preceding Tuesday which he rated at 2. On this "up-day" he
had had a successful day at work, played tennis and basketball and, after work, had gone out for a few beers with his co-
workers. When he remembered having played golf at 6:00
a.m., he changed his rating to a 1.

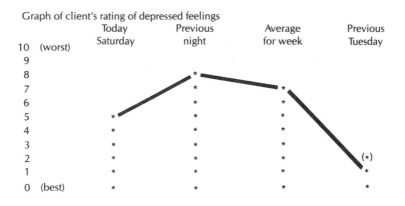

Graph of client's rating of depressed feelings

		Today	Previous	Average	Previous
		Saturday	night	for week	Tuesday
10	(worst)				
9					
8			*		
7			*	*	
6			*	*	
5		*	*	*	
4		*	*	*	
3		*	*	*	
2		*	*	*	(*)
1		*	*	*	*
0	(best)	*	*	*	*

The rating scale is deliberately "upside-down." This is designed to confuse the "up-down" metaphor (the bottom or 0 is equal to normal) and to introduce various shades of gray so that improvement and goal achievement is not set up as an all or nothing situation. In addition, this "upside-down" scale metaphorically makes getting better into a "down hill slide" whereas the reverse scale would make getting better into an "up hill battle." It seems important to end the technique with the description of an "up-day" even if it is a hypothetical one so that this getting better movement, the "down hill slide" is the last thing about the depressed feelings that the therapist addresses prior to taking some time out to consult with his or her team (if there is one) or to simply think about what to do.

At the end of the session, Mr. H was asked to predict, each night before going to bed, where on this scale the next day would fall. Then, at noon, he was to rate the day and to account for any differences between his prediction and the actual rating. He agreed to do this, saying "That makes sense."

Mr. H was given this prediction task because, throughout the session, the exceptions were described as spontaneous. As far as he could see, "up-days" were a matter of chance and there was nothing he could do about it. When he begins to account for any differences between his prediction and the actual rating, he might come to see that he does, in fact, have at least some control. The prediction tasks are designed to FIT with the randomness of spontaneous exceptions. Telling Mr. H to golf every morning at 6:00 a.m. would not have made sense to him since he did not see the golf as setting the mood for the day and therefore he could not see that he did indeed have some control. As long as the exception continues to be described as spontaneous, then tasks calling for specific behaviors that might serve as a trigger for the exception will usually not fit and, in fact, assigning such a task could only lead to what was called "resistance."

Mr. H's Report

Prediction	7	7	7	5	5	5	3
Actual	5	5	5	3	3	7	2

Mr. H could not account for the differences between predictions and ratings until the sixth day. On that day it rained and therefore he and his wife were unable to go jogging at 6:00 a.m. The jogging was something new for them to do together and, as a result of the scale, they decided to continue to have some physical exercise together before going to work. They made suitable arrangements for something to do when it rained.

Mr. H was satisfied with this way of deliberately inducing spontaneous "up-days" and thus therapy terminated with the second session.

Complaint = Feeling Depressed all the time
↓
Spontaneous Exceptions = Occasional "up-days"
↓
Differences between Complaint and Exception:

    "Up-days" included physical activities, smiling, and talking more with wife; being better organized at work
↓
PRESCRIBE: Predict random or spontaneous "up-days"

A chance meeting at a shopping center one year later revealed that occasional "down-days" were associated with three days or more when he did not have some physical activity early in the morning. He did not allow this to happen very often and is rather satisfied with the solution.

CASE EXAMPLE EIGHTEEN

Session 1

Mr. and Mrs. I and their two children, nine-year-old Becky and six-year-old Mary, came to therapy when Becky's misbehavior spread from home to school. At home they could cope with Becky's frequently behaving more like she is a five-year-old than behaving like a nine-year-old, but the teacher was "pulling her hair" over the escalating problem. Nothing either parent or the teacher tried helped in getting Becky to control her behavior and act her age. Sometimes Becky would lie on the floor, yelling and kicking with seemingly no provocation. Sometimes, however, when the parents expected this behavior Becky would control herself in spite of extreme provocation. These exceptions, however, happened no more than once in two weeks.

Nobody, it seemed, could account for the radical shifts in behavior and nobody could predict them. As mother put it, "It just don't make sense." Father was puzzled, mother was puzzled, the teacher was puzzled, the minister was puzzled, Becky and Mary were puzzled. So was the therapist.

Punishment did not work and, mother reported, neither did rewards. She had tried giving the girl points toward a special treat for every day she behaved, but she had never accumulated enough points.

In this case the exceptions were spontaneous and infrequent. Nobody could remember the most recent one, but they all could remember that there were spontaneous exceptions although none of them could describe Becky's good behavior or their behaviors that happened to coincide. Thus the team decided on a prediction-account for errors task.

"We are all impressed with your persistence and stick-to-it-iveness. It certainly must have been very frustrating at times and it must have made everybody angry, but – nonetheless – you have all maintained your hope and belief that there is a solution.

"Between now and next time we meet, we would like each

of you to predict each night before Becky goes to bed whether the next she will behave like an 8, 9, or 10 year old or if
she'll behave like a 5 or 6 year old. We would like you to do
this secretly and separately. Do not share your predictions
and do not talk about them. Then, next day, check out the
facts. If you were wrong in your prediction, figure out why
and if you are right, figure out why. Next time, we'll look at
all your predictions." (Therapist and parents then made sure
both children understood the task as well as they could.)

Session 2

Two weeks later, they reported a vast improvement.
Becky had shown some more mature behavior on at least
five days. Nobody had predicted more than one of these
except Becky who had always predicted more mature behavior. Mother, in contrast, had always predicted immature behavior because "I would rather be pleasantly surprised than
disappointed." Father's and Mary's predictions were also in-
accurate. Even in hindsight, nobody could account for any
of the better days. The mystery remained.

The therapist asked mother and father and Mary how
their behavior was different on these good days. Mary said
that she and Becky did not fight as much, which the parents
confirmed. The parents had seen no difference in their own
behavior. Becky thought that mother had been calmer on
those days, not complaining so much about her job. Mother
did not recall this difference.

Since a prediction task had seemed to prompt "better
days" more frequently, the team decided to give the family
the same task. They were concerned that nobody could account for or really describe the differences between good
days and bad.

Session 3

The good days had been more frequent in this two-week
period. Mother and Becky continued the same predictions
as they had during the previous period and dad's turned out

to be perfectly wrong. Becky had shown her more mature behavior on 9 of the 14 days. The sisters were not fighting on those days and the school also reported a vast improvement. Once again, nobody could account for the difference.

The team decided that they would once again give them a prediction task and decided to modify it so that each person would have some behavior that was contingent on Becky's spontaneously having a good day. In this way, perhaps the improvement good be built into some new family pattern of good days. Otherwise, if the good days remained random, then the bad days remained random and a "relapse" was probable.

"Between now and the next time, we would like you to continue predicting each day. But, we have something different to do for each of you. Mother, when your prediction is wrong (Becky has a good day), then we want you to spend some time with Becky doing something Becky likes doing. It doesn't need to be more than 15 minutes. Becky, when your prediction is right (you have a good day), then we want you to do something fun with your sister. Dad, whenever you are wrong in the right direction, that is, when you predict bad but it is good, we want you to do something fun with your wife." They all seemed to enjoy these additional tasks. (Mary was absent from this session.)

Session 4

The majority of days were good and they all found the tasks easy to do. Mother came to the conclusion that paying extra attention to Becky when she was good had always been a predictor for more good days, but she had not seen that until she had started on the homework task. Dad said he decided to forget making the predictions and just did more fun things with his wife and with his daughters. Becky said that her sister had been a bigger pain than usual, but she had played little kid games with her anyway.

At this point the family was confident that the problem was solved and the therapist and team decided to terminate therapy.

Six months later Mrs. I reported that Becky had started
lying and coming home late. Although this was different
misbehavior, mother was afraid it was the same problem
starting over again. The therapist asked what mother had
tried, but her response was unclear. He then asked if mother
had forgotten to spend at least 15 minutes a day doing plea-
surable things with her daughter. She had, but agreed it was
worth a try. The lying apparently stopped quickly and mother felt relieved.

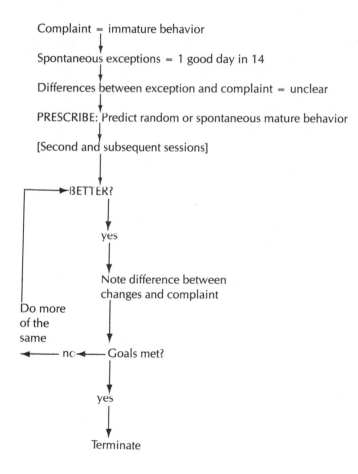

Complaint = immature behavior

Spontaneous exceptions = 1 good day in 14

Differences between exception and complaint = unclear

PRESCRIBE: Predict random or spontaneous mature behavior

[Second and subsequent sessions]

BETTER?

yes

Note difference between
changes and complaint

Do more
of the
same

no ◄── Goals met?

yes

Terminate

CASE EXAMPLE NINETEEN[2]

Session 1

Mrs. J came to therapy complaining that she had felt depressed for over three years. She had tried therapy twice previously, but had dropped out when there was no progress within a month or six weeks. She did not know if she was depressed about her marriage, her job, her age, or the fact that her youngest child (aged 19) was soon to marry and would be the last of the five to leave home.

"So tell me about the times when you feel the least depressed." Mrs. J seemed taken aback by this, saying that as far as she could tell, every day was alike. She dreaded getting up in the morning, dreaded going to work, dreaded going back home, dreaded going out even though she knew she should, dreaded coming back home, dreaded going to bed at night. "What do you dread least?" Mrs. J smiled slightly and said, "Sleeping, because then I don't know how bad things really are."

"If your husband were here, or your boss or your children, and I asked them about when you are least depressed, how would they answer?" She thought a long time about this before talking about her efforts to pretend to feel OK. She thought that she was able to fool her husband, boss and all her children except the youngest into thinking she was "up."

"What would it take to fool your youngest?" She did not know and believed this would be impossible, but—at my suggestion—agreed it might be worth an experiment. "Do you think that when your husband actually sees the real thing that he will realize that you have been fooling him?" She thought it would be clear to him because, when she was "up" over the years, she initiated sex. But she had not done this for over three years "but I would like to feel up to that."

During the break, I thought a lot about what to do. At that point there were no exceptions, deliberate or spontane-

---

[2]The therapy in this case was done without a team.

ous, although the "initiating sex" idea as a sign of solution might be thought of as a hypothetical solution. It seemed to be something she wanted, but suggesting she initiate sex did not seem to fit at this point because it was more of a result in her mind than a cause of the solution.

At this point, it seemed that the whole "I feel depressed" complaint was still rather global although a possible focal point had been developed around her "pretending to be 'up'" and fooling people.

"I am really impressed with how much you care about the feelings of other people and how well you can describe other people's behavior and attitude. But most of all, I was really struck with this pretending technique of yours but I am somewhat confused about how it works and how well it works. So, between now and next time, I want you to observe how close you come to really fooling people when you pretend to feel up."

Again, this task is rather similar to our formula first session task in that it asks her to observe the kinds of things she wants to see happen more often. Of course the task also suggests that she continue to do what she is already doing but focuses her on how well she fools other people rather than on her depressed feelings. Perhaps really fooling people would lead her to really fooling herself. Over the years many clients have reported that pretending to be "up" leads other people into thinking you are "up" and, therefore, treating you like you were "up," and then, as a consequence, you end up actually being "up."

Session 2

Two weeks later, Mrs. J reported that on three different days she thought she had really fooled her husband and might even have fooled her youngest on one of those days. She smiled a bit when she said that she had fooled Mr. J so well that she was afraid he was disappointed when she did not initiate sex. She had pretended to be up on ten different days, but felt that these three days were the only times she came close to fooling people. But she could not account for the differences between the three days and the other seven. Nor could she account for the differences between those ten days and the three days she had not felt up to pretending. She maintained that she had felt depressed throughout the interval, but that life was easier on the days she pretended.

The differences between

(1) really fooling people days;
(2) sort of fooling people days; and
(3) not trying to fool people days were not clear.

It all depended on how she felt when she got up in the morning and how other people responded to her efforts to fool them. Because of this randomness, a prediction task seemed called for.

"Well, I am certainly puzzled that some days, no matter how "down" you feel, you can fool people and other days you can really fool people into believing that you are 'up.'" "So am I." "Well, let's try an experiment. Each night, before going to bed, predict whether or not you will be able to really fool people the next day. Then, before you make the following day's prediction, account for any and all differences between your previous night's prediction and the results. Don't just go by your feelings, size up the reactions of your husband and your youngest child." She thought that we could probably learn something and agreed to the task.

Session 3

"I certainly better not take up betting on the horses. My ability to predict stinks."

Two weeks later Mrs. J reported that her predictions were never right. One night she predicted that she would not feel up to pretending the next day but, that next day, she ended up initiating sex with her husband! This was a shock, but a pleasant shock. So, she decided to predict that the next day she would fool everybody but she did not. However, she

could not account for this shift: it was a complete mystery
to her.

"How come? It certainly seems a reasonable prediction."

"Well, if I fooled anybody it was me. I really felt up. If I
was pretending at all I didn't know it." She gave up trying to
predict and just let each day happen as it might. Although
not really "up" during those 5 days, she was also not really
"down." I then asked her if that was OK with her, particularly if that would be true for most weeks in the coming six
months. It would be OK but not really satisfactory. Certainly not being really "down" or really "up" was far better than
being "really down."

Since Mrs. J is reporting that things are better, it calls for
some sort of message about doing more of whatever it is
that is working. It seemed to me that I needed to overcome
the temptation to do more or to do something different. The
intervention needed to involve doing more of the same of
what had worked.

"Now, I know you are really bad at predicting, but nonetheless I would like you to start predicting again even if you
are wrong every day. Each night, before going to bed, I
would like you to predict whether the next day you will
really fool yourself or other people. Right or wrong predictions do not matter at all. What I want you to notice is how
what other people do each day influences your prediction.

Session 4

"Last time when I left here I was really pissed. I really did
not want to make any more stupid predictions and I did not.
I decided I was through fooling people and just wanted to
get on with it." She had initiated sex with her husband on
two occasions and had felt better than "not up and not
down" and that feeling this way most days over the next six
months would be just fine. She wondered if I had deliberately made her pissed so that she would snap out of the depression. I honestly denied that intention and wished I had been
smart enough to figure that out because if I had I would

have done it in the first session. She laughed, "Nothing would have gotten me pissed then." She thought therapy was done and I wished her the best of luck as she left.

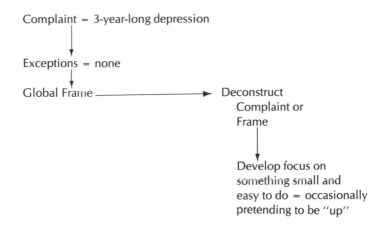

Complaint = 3-year-long depression

↓

Exceptions = none

↓

Global Frame ─────────────────→ Deconstruct
                                 Complaint or
                                 Frame

                                 ↓

                                 Develop focus on
                                 something small and
                                 easy to do = occasionally
                                 pretending to be "up"

HOW DO PREDICTION TASKS WORK?

At first glance having someone predict anything about the next day prior to going to bed seems rather absurd. At times, like with Mr. H, the results seems to suggest that the task is designed to help someone account for the "up-days" or the "better days" so that he or she can take control of his moods – to a greater or lesser extent. But what about those times when this does not occur?

Homework tasks including these absurd predictions implicitly include the therapist's predicting some improvement and, when the client follows through, he too implicitly acknowledges that a better day is possible. Perhaps this allows him or her to develop a self-fulfilling prophecy.

Implicit in our wondering about how these absurd prediction tasks work is the question about causation. Therapists and clients alike often assume that any problematic pattern is at least triggered if not caused by something that immediately precedes the pattern's occurrence. If this is a useful assumption, then it should be applied to non-problematic patterns as well. However, prediction tasks seem based on a different assumption.

Prediction tasks are based on the idea that what you expect to happen is more likely to happen once the process leading up to it is in motion. In pragmatic terms, this means that the prediction, made the night before, can sometimes be seen as setting in motion the processes involved in having a better day. No matter what guess the predictor puts down, the idea that he *might* have a good day is bound to cross his mind. Of course, having a good day is what he really wants and therefore a self-fulfilling prophecy might develop and this might prompt "better day behavior" the next day, right off the bat.

When someone consistently predicts better days, which might just be the expression of a wish or hope, it seems reasonable that they might then act to have better days and thus fulfill their wish. When someone consistently predicts bad days, there is the chance that they will surprise themselves and have a good day. Sometimes they will rebel against their prediction and force the good day pattern.

Prediction tasks are designed to FIT with the chancy nature of exceptions that are described as spontaneous. Since the clients do not perceive that any deliberate actions lead to or contribute to these exceptions, asking them to predict exceptions seems to make sense. Of course they are usually sure that bad days will continue unabated, but the implicit message *there will be good days* helps to create the expectation that good days will happen.

13

CONCLUSION

Up to this point the theory of solution has been looked at vertically for the similarities and differences that confirm the family resemblance among solution focused interviews. To a large extent, this approach has been dictated by the sequence of events during interviews. Perhaps the map is as simple a description as the variation between interviews allows. But to leave it at that — which might be the easy way out — is to suggest that this approach has cost some of us our highly valued simplicity. While this loss might represent an evolutionary swing from simplicity to complexity to simplicity, etc., it seems to me to be a call for Ockham's razor: What can be done with fewer means is done in vain with many.

EXCEPTIONS AS UNDECIDABLES

At first glance, the pathway that includes "deconstructing a global frame" may seem to bear little or no resemblance to the other pathways on the map. In fact, it may seem to be included in the family only because it is an option that is available to therapists should they not be able to help their client describe a viable exception. Although the therapist's "searching for exceptions" earmarks the pathway for family membership, the resemblance in this instance might make membership seem as tenuous as that between practicing basketball alone in your driveway and a chess game.

That is, the differences are more striking than any similarities and therefore one might think it better perhaps to visualize them as belonging to different families. In this case, family membership might be solely an artifact of the scope conditions.

Wider or broader scope conditions, which would allow for distinctions to be drawn that have nothing to do with what happens during the session, might classify the cases that follow this pathway as more strongly resembling some other family (i.e., "psychotic"). In this event, "deconstructing a frame" would be seen as more than an interviewing and intervention designing process: it would also serve to determine membership in this special family. However, other cases that fall under this particular extramural distinction readily fit on the map: Exceptions can be described that, when amplified, lead to a satisfactory solution. If simplification is possible, it must come from a different angle.

Looking at the theory horizontally or from a different angle reveals a similarity among the pathways that describing via the interviewing process or sequence of events has hidden away. What is hidden away is not beneath or behind the map. This concealment is due to the map's resemblance to a decision tree for interviewing and is essentially a result of its simplicity and familiarity.

Exceptions, undecidables, and the responses to the various tasks (behavioral and/or observational) are all designed to use the clients' ongoing experiences to change how they depict these experiences in the therapeutic situation. Each of the pathways represents a "dialect" within the therapeutic language game, an invention of the participants. When any of the pathways is successful, clients' depictions will change, the therapist will suggest doing more of the same, and a satisfactory solution is in the process of developing.

Described in this way, membership in the family of solution focused interviews is not at all dependent on using the map *as if* it were a decision tree and it is not dependent on the therapist's "searching for exceptions." These interpretations narrow down the theory and its usefulness. As Wynne

(1987) simply described it, a solution focus involves helping the client to "find the key to solution and then let them open the door for themselves and go from there" (p. 11). The central map, the theory construction methods, the interviewing style and techniques from which it was derived, is only one expression of the theory. It is certainly not the only way and it is not necessarily even the best way. It just happens to be the way my colleagues and I went about describing our descriptions of what is going on when we work with clients to develop solutions. This particular approach has a distinct advantage simply because it builds solutions that are within the clients' experiences.

PUZZLES

The purpose of this book has been to describe solutions and how client and therapist cooperatively develop them while staying within the scope conditions of the theory. Any description is only meant to be a picture-in-words while an explanation usually is an attempt to interpret (see behind or beneath) or to give a meaning (or meanings) to something. Throughout, the attempt has been to emulate Poe's purloined letter, to describe what is openly observable.

When we are puzzled about something, we are tempted to think that there are things hidden away. Yet frequently nothing of the sort is the case. It is not new "facts" that we want to know; all the "facts" lie open before us. The puzzle is created by our arrangement of the "facts" and by the idea that something lies behind.

How we describe what we see, what words we choose to describe the pictures, is based on how we construct the situation we are in as we observe the clinical events through the mirror or on videotape. Other constructions would use different words, thus different pictures would result. Not only do observers influence what they observe but, at least in human interaction situations, they help to create what they observe. For instance, once we got the idea that "every (complaint) rule has an exception" we started to ask clients about "what happens when the complaint does not?" which, in a very real sense, helped to create exceptions. As we know from years of practice, spontaneous mentions of exceptions are rare. Perhaps in real life (should an exception occur) it is seen as a "fluke" or it goes by unrecognized and, therefore, it is not a difference that makes a difference. Thus, if we had not asked, it is likely that clients would not have told us.

This leads to some interesting conundrums. For instance, between one-half and two-thirds of the time, first sessions include descriptions of exceptions. Does this say anything about real life problems (those not reported in a therapy situation) or does this only say something about the therapist and her client in the therapy situation? We cannot know for sure about real life since as soon as one asks about exceptions one creates the possibility of exceptions being described. Exceptions are not discovered, they are invented during the conversation between client and therapist. They are an element of a description, not a fact of real life.

This is not to say that "complaints," "exceptions," and "solutions" are any less *real* than "problems." It is only that the therapist participates in inventing the therapeutic reality. During therapy, the client talks about (or depicts) his real life problems which the therapist is attempting to influence that description by helping the client invent exceptions. When this goes well, subsequent sessions will include the client's depictions of real life changes. Even though therapists make the assumption that depictions are accurate pictures of real life, we cannot know for sure. All we can know is that the client is depicting things differently in session 2 than he was in session 1.

The various cases that have been described included complaints about cocaine abuse, alcohol abuse, hallucinations, depression, and physical violence, etc. However, the descriptions say little or nothing about "cocaine abuse" or "hallucinations" as such. The descriptions only describe the form of specific depictions within a constrained and limited setting. That is, the descriptions tell us that, whether the complaint involves "cocaine," or "hallucinations," or "spouse abuse," when therapist and client are able to invent exceptions and/ or increase the amount of change talk, solutions are possible. Reading the descriptions to say something about "cocaine abuse" as such is actually misreading and is beyond the scope of the theory and the descriptions themselves. At the risk of being redundant: such a misreading involves the breakdown of the distinction between map and territory.

What it does say, however, is that when therapists help their clients depict their real life problems in such a way that a similar description develops, then – even with a complaint like cocaine abuse or hallucinations – a solution can develop in which the client will say that things have changed. That is, the client will depict his real life situation without including cocaine abuse or hallucinations. This is, after all, exactly what therapists are after. Therapists and clients behave *as if* depictions were real life. Unfortunately, the *"as if"* is easily forgotten and such amnesia leads all too frequently to muddles of one sort or another.

DISCUSSION

Although the map and the expert systems seem to treat various alternatives as simple "yes or no" options and both are dependent on coherent "if, then" rules, many of the choices or rules are more recursive or interactive than is at first apparent. No matter how rigorous the rules may be, their application involves discretion and skill. After all, a map is just a representation or a presentation of a description. No matter how focused the therapist and client are, their conversation during a therapy session is not that constrained and is not as controlled as our depictions of it. That's the way it is with maps.

For instance, the decision, is this a visitor? complainant? customer? relationship needs to be made before any task can be assigned. Since this is not a "yes, no" choice based on a response to a single question or series of questions, but is a qualitative or evaluative description of a relationship, the answer is not always clear. Sometimes the best a therapist can say is that the relationship fits "more or less" well into one type rather than another. For instance, when the therapist cannot decide between complainant and customer, then even a well described exception (and/or hypothetical solution) might not be a suitable foundation for a behavioral task. It is best to be on the side of caution and assign an observational task, i.e., to deem the client-therapist relationship as falling into the complainant type. But, when the therapist can say that he or she is very confident that a client is a customer, then even an inadequately described exception (and/or hypothetical solution) can become usable as a foundation for a behavioral task.

The reverse is frequently true when the therapist cannot decide between visitor and complainant. Of course visitors have gripes, but their descriptions of them typically leave the impression that they are not in the therapist's office expecting anything to get better, i.e., they are not there for business purposes, they are just there because they have to be. If the therapist is confident in his or her description of this client as a visitor, then not giving a task is appropriate. However, if the therapist is unsure but leaning toward describing the client as a complainant, then an observational task, particularly the formula first session task, can be quite apropos.

How well the client's goal(s) is described can also influence this decision. In general, the better described the goal or the better described how the client will know when the problem is solved, the more confident the therapist can be in deciding that the client can be described as a "customer." Some hypothetical solutions (which are goals) are, in fact, well enough articulated that the therapist can decide that the client-therapist relationship is of the customer type and that the hypothetical solution can be handled *as if* it were a deliberate exception.

For brief therapy to be satisfactory, the present needs to be salient to the future. Otherwise, there is no sense in the client's doing something different or in seeing something differently. When the future, expressed in terms of goals, is drawn in specifics, i.e., in behavioral terms, and the goals are ones established by the client, then doing something now (in the present) to attain those goals makes sense. Goals need to be described in minimal terms, they need to be achievable and they need to be perceived by the client as difficult enough to demand effort.

Once exceptions (and/or hypothetical solutions) are seen by the client to make a difference and are seen as associated with the goal, then the present is clearly salient to the client's future and the client's task becomes the arduous one of making the exceptions into the rule.

No matter how poorly described the future is, its salience is primary. Without the expectation that things can get better, therapy makes no sense. In fact, the expectation that things can get better is the central presupposition behind all therapy.

REFERENCES

Bandura, A. & Schunk, D. (1981). Cultivating competence, self-efficacy, and intrinsic interest through proximal self-motivation, *Journal of Personality and Social Psychology, 41,* 586–598.

Barnlund, D. C. (1981). Toward an ecology of communication. In C. Wilder and J. H. Weakland (Eds.). *Rigor and Imagination: Essays from the legacy of Gregory Bateson.* New York: Praeger.

Berger, J., Fisek, M., Norman, R., & Zelditch, M. (1977). *Status characteristics and social interaction: An expectations state approach.* New York: Elsevier.

Brewster, F. (1985). Seeing Something. *Networker, 9*(6), 61–64.

Deci, E. (1975). *Intrinsic motivation.* New York: Plenum.

Deissler, K. (1986). *Recursive creation of information: Circular questioning as information production* S. Awodey (Trans.). Unpublished manuscript.

Dell, P. (1985). Understanding Bateson and Maturana: Toward a biological foundation for the social sciences. *Journal of Marital and Family Therapy, 11,* 1–20.

Derrida, J. (1981). *Positions.* Chicago: University of Chicago Press. A. Bass (Trans.).

de Shazer, S. (1978a). Brief hypnotherapy of two sexual dysfunctions: The crystal ball technique. *American Journal of Clinical Hypnosis, 20*(3), 203–208.

de Shazer, S. (1978b). Brief therapy with couples. *International Journal of Family Counseling, 6*(1), 17–30.

de Shazer, S. (1979a). On transforming symptoms: An approach to an Erickson procedure. *American Journal of Clinical Hypnosis, 22,* 17–28.

de Shazer, S. (1979b). Brief therapy with families. *American Journal of Family Therapy, 7*(2), 83–95.

de Shazer, S. (1982a). Some conceptual distinctions are more useful than others. *Family Process, 21,* 71–84.

de Shazer, S. (1982b). *Patterns of Brief Family Therapy.* New York: Guilford.

de Shazer, S. (1984). The Death of Resistance. *Family Process, 23,* 79–93.

de Shazer, S. & Molnar, A. (1984). Four useful interventions in brief family therapy. *Journal of Marital and Family Therapy, 10*(3), 297–304.

de Shazer, S. (1985). *Keys to solution in brief therapy.* New York: W. W. Norton.

de Shazer, S., Gingerich, W. J., & Weiner-Davis, M. (1985). Coding family therapy interviews: What does the therapist do that is worth doing. Presentation at *Institute for Research and Theory Development,* AAMFT Annual Conference.

de Shazer, S., Gingerich, W. J., & Goodman, H. (1987). BRIEFER: An expert consulting system. Presented at American Family Therapy Association Annual Conference.

de Shazer, S., Berg, I., Lipchik, E., Nunnally, E., Molnar, A., Gingerich, W., & Weiner-Davis, M. (1986). Brief therapy: Focused solution development. *Family Process, 25,* 207–222.

Dolan, E. (1985). *A path with a heart: Ericksonian utilization with resistant and chronic clients.* New York: Brunner/Mazel.

Erickson, M. H. (1954). Pseudo-orientation in time as a hypnotic procedure. *Journal of Clinical and Experimental Hypnosis, 2,* 261–283.

Erickson, M. H., Rossi, E., & Rossi, S. (1976). *Hypnotic realities.* New York: Irvington.

Feldman, L. & Pinsof, W. (1982). Problem maintenance in family systems: An integrative model. *Journal of Marital and Family Therapy, 8*(3), 295–308.

Fisch, R., Weakland, J. H., & Segal, L. (1983). *The tactics of change: Doing therapy briefly.* San Francisco: Jossey-Bass.

Fish, L. A. & Piercy, F. (1987). The theory and practice of structural and strategic therapies: A delphi study. *Journal of Marital and Family Therapy, 13*(2), 113–125.

Gingerich, W. J., de Shazer, S., & Weiner-Davis, M. (1987). Constructing change: A research view of interviewing. In E. Lipchik (Ed.). *Interviewing.* Rockville: Aspen.

Goffman, E. (1974). *Frame analysis.* New York: Harper & Row.

Goodman, H. (1986). BRIEFER: An Expert System for Brief Family Therapy. Unpublished Master's Thesis, University of Wisconsin-Milwaukee.

Goodman, H., Gingerich, W. J., & de Shazer, S. (1987). BRIEFER: An expert system for clinical practice. *Computers in Human Services,* (in press).

Gottman, J. (1979). *Marital interaction.* New York: Academic Press.

Haley, J. (1963). *Strategies of psychotherapy.* New York: Grune & Stratton.

Haley, J. (1967). (Ed.). *Advanced techniques of hypnosis and therapy: Selected papers of Milton H. Erickson.* New York: Grune & Stratton.

Haley, J. (1973). *Uncommon Therapy.* New York: W. W. Norton.

Haley, J. (1976). *Problem solving therapy.* San Francisco: Jossey-Bass.

Hofstadter, D. R. (1981). Analogies and roles in human and machine thinking. *Scientific American,* September, 1981. Revised and printed in D. R. Hofstadter, *Metamagical themas: Questioning for the essence of mind and pattern,* (1985), New York: Basic.

Keeney, B. (1983). *Aesthetics of change.* New York: Guilford.

Kim, J., de Shazer, S., Gingerich, W. J., & Kim, P. (1987). BRIEFER: An expert system for brief therapy. Paper presented at the IEEE Systems Man and Cybernetics Annual Conference, Alexandria, Virginia.

Kuhn, T. (1970). *The structure of scientific revolutions* (2nd ed.). Chicago: University of Chicago Press.

Latham, G., & Baldes, J. (1975). The "practical significance" of Lockes' theory of goal setting. *Journal of Applied Psychology, 60,* 122–124.

Lipchik, E. (1987). Interviewing. Rockville: Aspen.

Lipchik, E., & de Shazer, S. (1986). The Purposeful Interview. *Journal of Strategic and Systematic Therapies, 5*(1), 88–99.

Locke, E., Shaw, K., Saari, L., & Latham, G. (1981). Goal setting and task performance: 1969–1980. *Psychological Bulletin, 90,* 125–152.

Mead, G. H. (1934). *Mind, self and society.* Chicago: University of Chicago Press.

Miller, G. (1986). Depicting family trouble: A micro-political analysis of the therapeutic interview. *Journal of Strategic and Systemic Therapies, 5*(1), 1–13.

Molnar, A. & de Shazer, S. (1987). Solution focused therapy: Toward the identification of therapeutic tasks. *Journal of Marital and Family therapy, 13*(4), 349–358.

O'Hanlon, W. (1987). *Taproots: Underlying principles of Milton Erickson's therapy and hypnosis.* New York: W. W. Norton.

Shields, C. G. (1986). Critiquing the new epistemologies: Toward minimum requirements for a scientific theory of family therapy. *Journal of Marital and Family Therapy, 12*(4), 359–372.

Sluzki, C. (1983). Process, structure and world views: Toward an integrated view of systemic models in family therapy. *Family Process, 22*(4), 469–476.

Tomm, K. (1984). One perspective on the Milan systemic approach: Part I. Overview of development, theory and practice. *Journal of Marital and Family Therapy, 10*, 113–125.

Tomm, K. (1986). On incorporating the therapist in a scientific theory of family therapy. *Journal of Marital and Family Therapy, 12*(4), 373–378.

von Glasersfeld, E. (1975). Radical constructivism and Piaget's concept of knowledge. In F. B. Murray (Ed.). *Impact of Piagetian theory*. Baltimore: University Park Press.

von Glasersfeld, E. (1981). The concept of adaptation and viability in a radical constructivist theory of knowledge. In I. E. Sigel, D. M. Brodzinsky, & R. M. Goriuhoff, (Eds.). *New directions in Piagetian theory and practice*. Hillsdale: L. Erlbaum.

von Glasersfeld, E. (1984). An introduction to radical constructivism. In P. Watzlawick (Ed.). *The invented reality*. New York: W. W. Norton.

Watzlawick, P., Weakland, J. H., & Fisch, R. (1974). *Change*. New York: W. W. Norton.

Weakland, J. H. (1987). Personal communication.

Weakland, J. H., Fisch, R., Watzlawick, P., & Bodin, A. (1974). Brief therapy: Focused problem resolution. *Family Process, 13*, 141–168.

Weiner-Davis, M., de Shazer, S., & Gingerich, W. J. (1987). Using pretreatment change to construct a therapeutic solution: A clinical note. *Journal of Marital and Family Therapy, 13*(4), 359–363.

Wilder-Mott, C. (1981). Rigor and imagination. In C. Wilder & J. H. Weakland (Eds.). *Rigor and imagination: Essays from the legacy of Gregory Bateson*. New York: Praeger.

Winston, P., & Horn, B. (1984). *LISP*. 2nd edition. Reading: Addison-Wesley.

Wittgenstein, L. (1958). *The blue and brown books*. New York: Harper. R. Rhees (Trans).

Wittgenstein, L. (1968). *Philosophical investigations*. Revised Third Edition. New York: Macmillan. G. E. M. Anscombe. (Trans).

Wynne, L. (1987). Trying to create intimacy destroys it. *Family Therapy News*, April.

INDEX

197